HISTORY'S MYSTERIES

JIMMY BLACK

with Foreword by
JIMMIE MACGREGOR

SAINT ANDREW PRESS
EDINBURGH

Published by
SAINT ANDREW PRESS
121 George Street, Edinburgh EH2 4YN

Copyright © Jimmy Black 1993

ISBN 0 7152 0677 X

British Library Cataloguing in Publication Data
A catalogue record for this book
is available from the British Library
ISBN 071520677X

Illustrations on pages 5, 8, 9, 17, 21, 23, 32, 34, 35, 36(x3),
37, 66(x2), 68, 88, 92, 97, 102(x2), 118, 127, 138
from *The Comprehensive History of England* in 12 vols:
Macfarlane and Thomson, Blackie & Son's (1861).
Illustrations on pages 58, 59, 95, 113, 136 from *Old and
New Edinburgh* in 3 vols: James Grant, Cassell (1887).
Illustrations on pages 48, 56, 67, 100, 104, 128 from
Scottish Pictures: Green, Religious Tract Society (1891).
Illustration on page 88 from *The Scots Worthies*: J A Wylie
(ed), William Mackenzie (1880).
Illustration on page 83 from *The Church of Scotland: Past &
Present* in 5 vols: Robert Herbert Story (ed), William
Mackenzie (1890).
Illustration on page 43 from *Curious and Remarkable
Glasgow Characters*: Peter Mackenzie (1891).
Illustration on page 60 from *Literary Landmarks of Edin-
burgh*: Laurence Hutton, Osgood & McIlvaine (1891).
Illustrations on pages 142, 145 adapted from drawings by
Calum English.
Illustrations on pages 16, 120 by Lesley A Taylor.
Illustrations on pages 27, 135 by Michael Turnbull.

Design concept by Mark Blackadder.
Cover photograph by Paul Turner.
Inset photographs by Walter Bell.
Typeset in 11.5/14 pt Garamond.
Printed and **bound** by Athenaeum Press Ltd,
Newcastle upon Tyne.

CONTENTS

CONTENTS

CONTENTS

CONTENTS

FOREWORD
by
Jimmie Macgregor

WERE the Picts permanently pickled?
How did an elephant find its way on to
Dumbarton's coat of arms? Did Highland
cattle really change colour from black to
ginger, and why is 'foolscap' so-called?
Many such questions are posed here and
very few are answered, but Jimmy Black
sets his riddles in such a diverting manner
that solutions would be an anti-climax.

My first meeting with Jimmy was in
the 'Macgregor's Gathering' studio of BBC
Radio Scotland, and immediately after our
talk I rushed into the producer's office
screaming, 'We must have him back!' We
did, and more than 80 appearances later
Jimmy was still delivering the goods in the
series which we came to call 'History's
Mysteries'.

Jimmy Black is the most affable of men:
a natural raconteur with an insatiable
curiosity, a retentive memory and a hearty
sense of humour. Our radio set pieces
always over ran and Jimmy would still be
talking long after the microphones were

switched off. Following the story of Luggie Jean, the lady with three ears, there was much unbroadcastable speculation about the location of the extra lug and social problems arising therefrom.

Jimmy asks what would have happened if Queen Victoria had married the young guards officer who had won her affections before Albert appeared. We hear about the wonderful musical bedpost, and learn that Robinson Crusoe was such a pain in the neck that a real man Friday would probably have drowned him.

There are 60 such stories here, told in the relaxed and eminently enjoyable style of Jimmy Black. The tales transfer effortlessly from the microphone to the printed page, making *History's Mysteries* an irresistible read.

INTRODUCTION
by
Jimmy Black

HISTORY is a thing of the past, say the cynics. But the human race goes on making history, and does not seem likely to lose its enthusiasm for the activity.

Scots have always been prolific history-makers. They have been making it to their own jealously-guarded recipe ever since they became recognised by the rest of the world as a nation.

Alas, the Scots suffer from a kind of nervous combination of pride and guilt about the history made by their ancestors. They feel in some way responsible for it. Consider the scene reported to have been witnessed in a Falkirk pub. A discussion was taking place, over several rounds of pints, on the subject of the defeat of WILLIAM WALLACE in the first Battle of Falkirk. At a point far into the conversation, a man called LACHIE drew himself up to his full height (four feet seven) and in a voice vibrating with emotion, he declared, 'See if Ah had been there, it wid hiv been a diff'rent story!'

Outside observers fool themselves into

believing that they can decipher the peculiar recipe of Scottish history. Certainly it contains elements of courage, daftness, greed, madness, genius, saintliness and sordidness, but in what proportions? Ah, there the experts are left guessing and arguing among themselves.

Two other ingredients used in certain variations of the main recipe, confuse the puzzled pundits—kidology and mystery. Many Scots sprinkle liberal measures of these fascinating garnishings into their history-making—often without realising it. The Scottish history so produced have provided the tit-bits gathered together in this book.

The reader may consider this book as a stroll through a forest of question-marks. On the way are encounters with a joker who may have kidded OLIVER CROMWELL ... ROBINSON CRUSOE's role model ... Queen VICTORIA's Scottish boyfriend (not the one you think!) ... American news-flashes through a bedpost ... a girl with three ears ... only a few of a scattering of oddments and oddities.

Questions are fascinating and answers often boring. Isn't it nice, just sometimes, that there are no answers to deflate the soufflé of historical mystery?

ACKNOWLEDGMENT

The Author would like to acknowledge with thanks the many and diverse sources for the tales within this book—the people and the ancient books too numerous to mention.

AIRSHIP

CRASHES
IN
FLAMES.

WHAT
GOT
INTO THE
BEDPOST?

IN the late 1930s, a man called MIDGE worked as an unskilled labourer on the building of the Riddrie Cinema in Glasgow. He was clearly a man of many skills. The way he organised his part of the building site was quite something—deploying the materials to save double-handling, calculating just how much of each item was needed for an operation, and protecting his materials from the weather.

He certainly seemed a quiet, level-headed chap, not given to the excesses of most of his colleagues.

Some of his personal history became known only gradually to those few on site with whom he would chat at break-time. Apparently his family were travelling people, which explains how Midge acquired his skills, but he had chosen a spell of static city life for a change.

One day, he told the story of his Uncle JEM who, with his wife and son, had also decided to settle in one place. Jem took over and renovated a derelict cottage in what was then a remote area some distance from Edinburgh. Having roughed it around Scotland for many years, Jem and his wife decided to go for what, to them, would be the ultimate in luxury—a big brass bedstead with soft mattress, pillows, sheets and blankets. Going to bed was now sheer bliss!

After a few weeks, Jem told Aggie, his wife, that he was being wakened some mornings, around about two or three, by strange sounds coming from the brass bedpost at his head. When he put his ear to the bedpost, he could hear news and music from a radio station called 'Schenectady' in New York!

Aggie said she had heard nothing because she always slept like a log—but, anyway, Jem was acting daft and having her on! She and their son, young Jem, laughed their heads off at Dad and told him to stop being ridiculous!

Well, Jem got quite angry at that and challenged them to stay awake with him that night to listen in. They turned him down flat! This put Jem in the huff for a few days.

However, one very memorable morning in early May 1937, Jem had something awful to report. He was able to tell Aggie and young Jem that, during the night, he had heard news on the bedpost that the

German airship 'Hindenburg' had caught fire at Lakehurst Airport, New Jersey—and 36 people had been killed!

How could that be? There was no radio in that cottage, the nearest neighbour was miles away and they did not see any newspapers until later in the day—when Jem's story was proved to be true!

Jem had no other way of knowing what happened to the 'Hindenburg'. How did that broadcast get into the bedpost? Was it really coming from there or did Jem have some special gift?

Midge certainly believed the bedpost story, but he never found anyone who could explain convincingly how a bedpost became a radio ....

A CONSORT
FROM
CUMBERNAULD?

FOR over five centuries, the FLEMINGS of Cumbernauld elbowed their way into the stories of Scottish history. However, the name might have died out in the eighteenth century if Lady CLEMENTINA FLEMING had not married the tenth Lord ELPHINSTONE of Carberry Tower.

In 1799, her grandson, CHARLES ELPHINSTONE, took over the Fleming estate, and he came to live at Cumbernauld House, calling himself ELPHINSTONE-FLEMING. His achievements included becoming an Admiral, MP for Stirlingshire, and a much-loved head of the local gentry. Charlie's son, Lieutenant-Colonel JOHN ELPHINSTONE-FLEMING, inherited the title of Lord Elphinstone from his cousin John in 1860.

Years before then, this cousin John figured in the most intriguing story ever linked with the Fleming family. It appears that cousin John had also followed an army career. Young Captain Elphinstone of the Horse Guards, a dashing, handsome, clever man, caught the eye of King WILLIAM IV and soon became a favourite at Court.

He also caught the eye of the King's niece, Princess VICTORIA. The young couple took such a fancy to each other that their mutual fondness became the talk of the town. Love was certainly in the air—and if they had married, what different deeds and dynasties might have made history?

Fate, however, decided that our history would be different— William's sudden death in 1837 set that young girl off on her long reign as Queen Victoria. Her romance with John survived a further week or two, but then, with breathtaking swiftness, the Captain was dispatched to Madras in India, to be Governor. He served with distinction, but in obscurity. It was as if the Court of St James back in England had never heard of him. John Elphinstone never married.

The young VICTORIA *[after* WINTERHALTER]

After a decent passage of time, the Queen married Prince ALBERT of Saxe-Coburg and Gotha—a love match.

But on hot Indian evenings, out on the terrace, did the Governor of Madras yearn for his lost love? Did the Queen Empress remember those carefree hours with her gallant Captain? Did they ever pass secret messages to each other? History refuses any answers ....

WHATEVER HAPPENED TO 'DRIBBLE DRONE'?

MINISTERS have always been targets for criticism. Modern ministers say, rather philosophically, 'Well, it's better than being ignored!' Long ago, though, some ministers would have rejoiced at being ignored. Take 'DRIBBLE DRONE', for instance. This story is constantly repeated up by the Cromarty shore about a cleric who is known only by that nickname (which speaks volumes).

A few years after the Reformation, as a candidate for the pulpit of the East Kirk in the town, 'Dribble' had to preach a trial sermon. That Sunday morning, ALEXANDER, nephew of the then Earl of SEAFIELD, set off for church. He was a pupil of the local Cromarty School and recognised by his schoolmasters as an aristocratic delinquent! His wild behaviour was a blight on the town; and some of his teachers, having endured this lad, fell victim to that malady which today is called a nervous breakdown!

So there he was, that Sunday morning, dressed in the school uniform of jacket, breeches, white stockings and cocked hat,

and strutting like a peacock, when he
noticed a hole in one of his stockings.

Rather cleverly he gathered some white,
prickly seed-cases—'burrs' in Scotland—
from a bush, and he clipped them across
the hole to hide it.

The service, and 'Dribble's' sermon,
passed without incident and Alexander was
just leaving the kirk with a young lady on
his arm. An old worthie, just behind him,
noticed the vegetation on his stocking and
cried, 'Alex! There's a burr on your stocking
—I'll pull it off!' The man bent down and
Alex unreasonably kicked his hand away!

Angered, the old fellow clobbered the
young aristocrat with a right hook! One
punched led to another, other members of
the congregation joined in, and soon a full-
scale barney was roaring through the kirk!

Later, questions were asked. Was the
attempted removal of the burr truly the
catalyst which set off a huge explosion of
bad temper? Or was there a cauldron of
resentment bubbling away under a thin
covering of respectability—the resentment
of kirk members at having to listen to the
dreary droning of the minister, 'Dribble'?
Was the slightest excuse going to make it
boil over anyway?

'Dribble' himself seems to have faded
from the annals of the parish ....

DID
GOOD QUEEN BESS
REALLY PICK
JAMIE?

THE absolute monarch of centuries ago seemed to have had the prerogative of choosing a successor. When ELIZABETH I of England was getting on a bit, her thoughts turned to her successor.

Would she pick the daughter of PHILIP of Spain, a legitimate claimant, or one of the descendants of two of HENRY VIII's sisters? Or would she pick JAMES VI of Scotland?

Bess refused to name anybody, since it was quite within the bounds of possibility that the supporters of the one she chose would try to hasten their candidate on to the throne by the use of some little device—such as her assassination!

But in March 1603, when her death seemed imminent, CECIL, her secretary, and Lord-Admiral HOWARD, her favourite, pressed her for an answer to the burning question.

Sir WILLIAM CECIL
[*after* VERTUE]

Certainly James VI of Scotland had played his cards pretty astutely, keeping in

with the lady, even though she had not been too kind to his mammy, MARY Queen of Scots—Elizabeth had ordered Mary's execution some years before.

Elizabeth said to her courtiers that a *king* must follow her. The King of France, they asked? She remained silent. And when they mentioned James, she turned her face to the wall and said nothing … the ladies-in-waiting confirmed this.

ELIZABETH I
[after
ZUCCHERO]

Regardless, as far as the ruling group of courtiers were concerned, James was still the safest bet. Indeed, later they told the tale of how, just before she died, they again mentioned James to the coma-tose Queen. On the speaking of Jamie's name, Bess arose in her bed. Looking round to Cecil and Howard, she is said to have waved her arms about, forming the shape of a crown. Those two politicians, by some form of mutual, lateral thinking, deduced that she had thus chosen James of Scotland to take the throne of a United Kingdom.

But did she really chose James as her successor? Or was she just trying to say to Cecil and Howard, as well as she could, 'Get lost!' Did those two make the whole story up? The mystery is still there for them to hide behind ....

THE
MYSTERIOUS
WEEKEND

THE mysterious weekend in question was
spent by NEVILLE CARDUS in London. The
great writer on cricket and music was
invited to stay at the home of a Scotsman.
He was reporting on a Test Match at the
Lords cricket ground for the *Manchester
Guardian* and so it was convenient to accept
this kind invitation from no less a person
than J M BARRIE, author of the classic tale
Peter Pan.

Barrie's home, Adelphi Terrace House,
seemed an odd place. The man servant,
THURSTON, was ghostlike and dressed himself in a brown, brass-buttoned uniform.
Cardus certainly raised an eyebrow when he
discovered, as the weekend went on, that
the man could speak several languages and
revealed an expertise on classical Greece! It
was hard to believe that he was real—yet,
he pressed Neville's jacket and trousers
every day and was the perfect butler.

After Cardus had been in the house a
few hours, Barrie suddenly appeared, filling
the room with thick pipe smoke and

coughing and spluttering endlessly! He exchanged a few pleasantries with Cardus and then vanished for two days.

Thurston served Neville's meals. He dined alone, except on Saturday night, when a woman in a dressing-gown joined him at table. She turned out to be Barrie's sister, and invited Neville to a musical evening in her boudoir! She played the piano and sang, although her voice, from Neville's description, resembled Rene's wife in the BBC comedy series, '*Allo! Allo!*' —tuneless and loud.

Later, a dinner-suited young man came in unannounced, chatted about Neville's cricket reports and then left without saying goodbye or leaving his name.

Following this series of surprises, Cardus was shocked when he went into the bathroom. It was a shambles! Shaving-brushes seemed to be growing all around it— decorated with congealed soap! Rusty razor-blades lay around like a minefield, with filthy towels draped everywhere! Was this the bathroom of a much-respected writer with a super-efficient butler!?

Barrie finally re-appeared to wish Neville farewell, who left, wondering, had this weekend been real? Or was this some bizarre rehearsal for a Barrie play … ? Cardus never found the answer.

IT COULD
HAVE BEEN
ROUGH
FOR FRIDAY

WHAT a barney broke out in November 1701 at the SELCRAIGE household in Largo! ALEXANDER, one of three sons, had bashed the rest of the family about, simply because when he had mistakenly taken a drink from a glass of salty water, somebody laughed!

The whole family—mum, dad and the three sons—were made to appear before the kirk session. Alexander, himself, was made to stand alone before the pulpit to repent of his particularly outrageous behaviour.

The SELCRAIGES were also known as the SELKIRKS. And the obstreperous son went to sea, known as ALEXANDER SELKIRK. In a year or so he was navigator aboard a ship called 'The Cinque Ports' on an expedition to the South Seas.

There are different versions of what happened when the ship anchored off the island of Juan Fernandez. One says that, after a blazing row with the captain, Alex was dragged into a small boat, put ashore on the island and left there as the ship sailed off. Another says that the narky Largo man actually asked the captain to put him off at the island. The master of the ship was only too willing to oblige, knowing that Alexander was quite capable of causing a row on an empty island! Whatever the case, Alexander was surrounded by a lot of salt water for some 52 months.

He was finally rescued by the British Navy and became a mate on 'HMS Weymouth'. That was the ship he died on —another mystery, or so it seems.

Alexander Selkirk never got on with his fellow humans. Perhaps he had a personality defect in an age when there were no 'shrinks' available to stretch him on a couch. And, if he had been normal, would he have lived a quite different life, thus denying the author DANIEL DEFOE of the plot of his famous novel *Robinson Crusoe*? And if there had been a character on Juan Fernandez like Crusoe's Friday, would poor Friday, after suffering the stroppy Scot for so long, have rushed into the sea and gone swimming over the horizon?

Mystery still hides the real truth about Alexander Selkirk.

WHO
SET
THE FIRE?

ST MARY'S Parish Church in the hamlet
of Whitekirk, near Haddington, really is a
white kirk. Its history goes back more than
1500 years.

The saint, BALDRED of Lindisfarne
preached here beside a healing well. It is
also said that AENEAS SILVIUS POCCOLOMINI,
an Italian cleric who was saved from ship-
wreck in the North Sea in 1430, walked
barefoot for ten miles through the snow to
give thanks for his deliverance at the
White Kirk. He later became Pope PIUS II.

It was, of course, one of the quaint little
ways of English armies to pillage places like
St Mary's Kirk. They did not overlook the
bonny white-washed building. It was one
of their favourite targets.

But mystery surrounds what happened
at St Mary's on the 26th February 1914. On
that day the kirk was put to the torch by a
person or persons unknown! Astonished
villagers turned out to quench the flames,
asking each other who on earth would want
to burn this beautiful place of worship,

sitting among the quiet, friendly fields of East Lothian? It wasn't the English army this time!

When the fire was extinguished, the search for clues began and, behind the church, two pieces of paper were found. On one was written: *'By torturing the finest and noblest women in the country, you are driving more women into rebellion.'*

The other piece of paper warned the Prime Minister, and then Home Secretary REGINALD MCKENNA, to stop the forcible feeding of women prisoners under what was known as the 'Cat and Mouse Act'.

So, it appeared that the Suffragettes did the deed, but no clues were left to identify the culprit or culprits. A hammer and knife were also found, but they were of no value in the investigation.

Did some gentlewomen Suffragette sympathisers living in the district, certain that they would never be suspected of such a crime—did *they* go out to the White Kirk with the matches and oily rags? Or was it travelling supporters of the cause? Or did some evil-minded misogynist light the fire and leave false clues to throw the blame on those great women crusaders?

The kirk was beautifully restored. But the truth of events on that February night in 1914 will never be known.

Charles. P.

WHATEVER HAPPENED TO CHARLIE'S GOLD?

STORY after story has claimed to tell the true tale of Bonnie Prince CHARLIE's gold, sent from France to fund his Rebellion. A favourite is the one that begins in the Jacobite town of Montrose.

In 1745, as the English attacked Lord OGILVY's Jacobite forces at Brechin, they also had a warship bombarding Montrose. Another English warship was coming up to join the fun when, out of the mist, a French ship sailed in to play chases with it!

Just then, with perfect timing, one of Ogilvy's men Captain ERSKINE of Dun— rushed in with his squad to turn the town guns on that first English man-o'-war, 'The Hazard', forcing it to surrender!

The captured ship was then renamed 'The Prince Charles' and sent off to France to collect badly-needed funds for financing the young Chevalier's uprising.

Bonnie Prince CHARLIE

A motley crew of Irish and French sailors brought the vessel, with a hefty casket of

gold and precious stones, all the way back and up round the North of Scotland, heading for a secret rendezvous. Alas, units of the English navy gave chase! The Prince Charles ran for cover into the Kyle of Tongue and the captain beached his craft.

The crew fought off an English landing party for as long as they could, then scarpered inland.

From this point, the plot gets tacky! Their speed of escape was, of course, hampered by having to carry that box of goodies, so they dumped it into a small loch.

The Prince had sent the MCKENZIES to collect the dosh, but, here's the rub. Nobody could identify the wee loch it had been dumped into! Lochs are scattered all over the place in that part of the country. On the map, they look like blue confetti! A stranger could hardly tell one from another.

It is said that the treasure was never recovered, but questions linger. Could the crew have fibbed about not remembering which loch the casket sank into? Did they keep the loot? Or is that priceless fortune still snuggling beneath the chill waters of some loch, its location known only to the fish? Or has somebody retrieved it and laughed all the way to the piggy bank?

WHAT
BECAME OF
THE ANGEL
OF MERCY?

SPRING was in the West of Scotland air on the evening of Thursday, March 13th 1941. That evening had *just* the hint of a chill to it. The sky was clear all the way to Venus and back, and the whole area was bathed in the ghostly light of the full moon. It was a Bomber's Moon.

It is difficult to remember which was heard first—the throbbing of the bombers' engines or the air-raid alert siren. But, not long after 'black-out' time, everybody in Glasgow and the towns around the city, knew that, somewhere along Clydeside, death and destruction would rain down from those throbbing engines.

In an hour or so, it became known that the prime target for the bombers this time was the Clydebank area.

There was the full range of human reactions on that desperate night. The one that is remembered most and longest is incredible, preposterous, glorious courage. One example is still talked of.

Just before midnight, a young girl

walked into the Radnor Park Church Hall. It was being used as a temporary casualty station and the floor was strewn with injured people. Just about then the bombing was reaching a hellish intensity.

The girl asked if there were any medical personnel in the hall. When the answer was 'no', she lifted an injured baby and rushed out of the station.

It seems that, earlier in the evening, she had jumped on to an ambulance near Giffnock where she lived. It was heading for Clydebank and she, being a student nurse, was heading for the same place.

With the baby in her arms, she now commandeered that same ambulance and demanded that the driver take them to Glasgow's Western Infirmary—a nightmare journey indeed!

At the Western, she made sure the baby was in good hands and then asked the medical students, who were on air-raid duty, to come back with her to Clydebank. Six of them did.

En route their ambulance was blasted onto its side. Undaunted, they hauled it upright and found it to be still driveable, so they all got to Clydebank. In the hours that followed, that student nurse and those medical students really graduated to the top ranks of their noble profession. After the miracles they performed that night, they could certainly consider themselves fully qualified!

Many people received honours for their devotion to duty during the Clydebank Blitz. But not that student nurse. Nobody had time to ask her name. And she didn't have time to tell them. So, who was she? Whatever happened to that angel of mercy?

GETTING
DOWN TO
BRASS
TACKS

THEY tell some rare tales in the Black Isle.
And the tales often have twists in their tails.

The Ferintosh estate in the Parish of
Urquhart, which was once owned by the
famous DUNCAN FORBES of Culloden, had a
community in the seventeenth century
which was as paranoid about witches as any
other community in the country at that
time.

Four poor women in Ferintosh were
identified as witches in 1662. It was
decided that their witchery had to be
verified by a recognised witch-tester.
About that time, a person called PATERSON
was making a fat living travelling around
Scotland testing women accused of witchcraft. This Paterson came to the Black Isle
and the four Ferintosh women were submitted for testing along with another 14 from
Strathglass.

The hair was shaved from their heads
and they were stripped naked so that
Paterson could rub some kind of oil all over
their bodies. Then this witch-tester pressed

a brass tack into some part of the body of each lady. It is said that not one of them cried out in pain!

They were then ordered by Paterson to find where the tacks had been inserted. If a woman failed to locate where in her body the tack had been stuck, this was taken as clear evidence that she was, indeed, a witch!

It can only be imagined what desperate, frantic contortions those poor souls put themselves through trying to find where the brass tacks had pierced them!

It is just about this point that the tale disappears into the tunnel of mystery, for it is not recorded whether any or all of the women managed to find and extract those tacks. Therefore, nobody knows if they were ever confirmed as witches.

Further, Paterson had always been assumed to be a man, but was later found to be a *woman*!

So, what became of the Ferintosh lassies? And in this brass tack business, had they perhaps been subjected to the practice of Scotland's first woman hypnotist? No one on the Black Isle seems to know ....

THE MYSTERY
OF THE
KING'S
BIG TOE!

WHAT a splendid affair it was when King
GEORGE IV, with all the adornments of
majesty, arrived on his great State visit to
Edinburgh in August 1822—the first royal
visit since the '45 Rising.

The King was not popular in Scotland
at that time. The Scots were upset by the
dreadful treatment he had meted out to his
queen, CAROLINE, wrongfully accusing her
of infidelity. Nonetheless, when he
announced his visit, the news went to the
heads of some Scots like intoxicating liquor
and people from all over Scotland planned
to squeeze into Edinburgh during those
hectic weeks in August. (Incidentally
much of the big show was stage-
managed by Sir WALTER SCOTT.)

Of course, the 'Second City of
the Empire', Glasgow, could not
be outdone in the matter of wel-
coming the King to Scotland. Lord
Provost ALSTON and his 'cooncillors'
invited the King to nip over to Glasgow
for a visit. The King replied that there

GEORGE IV
[after
Sir T LAWRENCE]

wouldn't be time in his tight itinerary for this, but he was so pleased to be asked that he ordered Sir THOMAS LAWRENCE, the great artist, to paint a portrait of his good self, the King, and send it to Glasgow City Hall. That portrait never arrived ....

Undeterred by their invitation being rejected, the Lord Provost, 'cooncillors' and magistrates decided to visit the King in the capital instead. They were all given lessons on how to conduct themselves before His Majesty and off they went, having spent £1000, dressed like the cast of a Cinderella pantomime!

Funny things happened on that trip, according to the cooncillors' report on their return. For instance, they were told that, in the King's presence, they should walk with their right hands to the wall! It was also claimed that when they lined up on the Royal Yacht in Leith Roads to be presented to His Majesty, every one of them was required to kiss the King's big toe! On his royal right foot!

Reflection after the Edinburgh trip gave rise to thoughts of whether the King had been having some royal fun at the expense of the Glasgow folk. However, obviously still miffed, later in his life the Lord Provost turned down, rather disdainfully, the King's offer of a knighthood!

WHO KILLED 'LUGGIE' JEAN?

THE nineteenth century was drawing to its last years when it brought one dreadful morning to the village of Cumbernauld. Shock quivered through the place as local people heard the awful news. 'LUGGIE' JEAN had been found dead in a water-hole on the edge of Fannyside Moor.

Villagers had a special affection for JEAN LINDSAY because she was regarded as being different from anyone else in the whole world. You see, Jean had been born with *three* ears—hence her nickname 'Luggie' Jean. (It is not recorded exactly where that third ear was located.)

Jean was a servant lass to a well-to-do family in the village and it was at their house that Cumbernauld's only policeman began his investigations. He proved himself to be a veritable 'Poirot'!

The constable checked the movements of all his suspects around the time of Jean's death. His attention to detail was remarkable. And he even brought in the experts with the state-of-the-art forensic techniques to examine the area around that water-hole.

Within days, the man who employed Jean was charged with her murder. His trial began at Edinburgh's High Court. However, the long procession of witnesses through the court produced volumes of conflicting evidence that turned the trial into something of an entertainment. But it was the two star witnesses who performed the grand finale, for they they produced a classic Glasgow *versus* Edinburgh encounter.

The forensic expert for the prosecution was a Professor of Glasgow University and his counterpart for the defence was a Professor of Edinburgh University. The defence claimed that Jean had drowned herself, while the prosecution averred that her employer had drowned her.

What a brilliant display of thrust and parry those two put on! Their arguments sounded so clever and convincing that the poor jurors, left in a fair tizzie, ultimately, returned that peculiarly Scottish verdict of 'Not Proven'.

The mists of mystery still shroud this case. Did Jean really kill herself? Or was she killed by someone who believed that a girl with three ears must be a latter-day witch? Or did her employer really kill her?

The case continues … ?

WAS THE PRIEST THE OLD SCOTTISH OUTLAW?

IN the appendix to *Rob Roy*, Sir WALTER SCOTT recounts a tale told to him by a friend who had travelled in France.

The traveller had been invited to watch a procession from the window of an apartment in a Paris back street. The flat was occupied by an old gentleman who appeared to be a Benedictine priest.

After the parade had passed, the visitor chatted to the tall, thin, gaunt cleric. They were speaking, in French, of the marvels of architecture in the French capital, when the old priest said, with a suddenly strong Highland accent, that none of these wonders of Paris were worth the High Street of Edinburgh!

He then revealed that he was ALLAN BRECK STEWART, living in Paris on a small army pension. He also said that he had joined a monastery.

The visitor was astonished, and a little alarmed, that he was actually speaking to the foster-son of one JAMES STEWART who

Sir WALTER SCOTT

had been hanged for the murder of the Red Fox, COLIN CAMPBELL of Glenure, in the notorious Appin murder in 1742. After all, it was generally believed that Stewart had been the innocent scapegoat and that Allan Breck was the real murderer who had fled to the continent.

The consensus of opinion on Sir Walter Scott's version of the story was that it was phoney. In recent years though, there has been some remarkable detective work done by the Irish teacher and writer, SEAMUS CARNEY.

He discovered that no monastery in France records Breck as a member, but it is possible that he went to a Paris college as a lay brother. Carney did, however find the following name in a French reference book of old military pensioners—ALLAN STUART D'ARTOURY. There is certainly no place in France called 'Artoury', but was it perhaps a corruption of Ardtur, in Appin, where Breck hid after Culloden? Was the twist in the name a rather cheeky cover-up?

Maybe Scott's friend really did meet the man thought to have been the murderer of the Red Fox back in the mid-eighteenth century. If so, does Allan Breck Stewart lie in a Paris grave? An intriguing thought.

TEN PAST SEVEN:
AN ODD
WITCHING
HOUR

IN the big band era of the 1930s, every lad worth his salt, even if he could only wheeze a tune from a mouth-organ, dreamed of playing with AMBROSE or ROY FOX, JACK PAYNE or even the legendary PAUL WHITE-MAN. Those who couldn't play any instrument probably dreamed of singing with such a top-bill dance band.

Of the aspiring singers of that time, would anybody remember HAROLD who hailed from Coatbridge? Perhaps not many. Yet he had girls clamouring just to *touch* him when he sang with a wee band called The Masqueraders, at Friday late night dances in the halls of the West of Scotland. This was in the days long before girls began screaming at Frank Sinatra, never mind The Beatles.

Harold's voice was mellifluously baritone, and his rendition of the old favourite 'Stardust' was regularly described as out of this world! It was confidently expected that he would, in time, move up the league of dance-band singers.

There was, however, some doubt among his closest friends. Harold was a building-trade worker, and those who knew him on the sites swore that, during the week, the singer's voice sounded more like a circular saw than a mellifluous crooner! Even his speaking voice grated on the ears of those within earshot! It was strong, right enough —but rough! How then, could the lad sing like RUDI VALLEE on Friday nights?

So what was the secret of Harold's success? His best pal told how, after the singer was washed and dressed, ready for a Friday night before his public, his granny, with whom he lived, would mix up what she called Harold's 'ginger'. (Now, 'ginger' was a local word in the West of Scotland for *all* soft drinks. It did not mean that any actual ginger had been used in the preparation.)

Granny gave Harold this drink at precisely seven o' clock and he would sit quietly until ten past seven. Soon he was off to whichever *palais de danse* was lucky enough to welcome The Masqueraders that night. And soon his rich baritone would fill the hall with its velvety music ....

It was said that by Saturday, if Harold didn't have a booking, his voice returned to a sound more like Donald Duck.

Nevertheless, for years Harold remained

the darling of the dancers in the West of Scotland night spots.

This potion Harold swallowed each week was said to have been made by his granny from secret ingredients—the types and proportions of which were passed on to her by her great-grandmother. Granny didn't pass on the details of the mixture to Harold before she died. And, with the old lady away, Harold simply stopped singing. His career was over.

So, what was in that 'ginger'? Would it ever be possible to mix it up again?

A' FOR
PRINCE
CHERLIE

FALKIRK seemed like the centre of the universe in January 1746, when the armies of Prince CHARLES EDWARD STUART and the English General HAWLEY were lining up to do battle.

In the morning, before the clash, a strange little *tête-á-tête* took place at Callendar House in the town, between General Hawley and the beautiful (and clever) Countess of KILMARNOCK.

They took tea together, chatted, and altogether enjoyed a pleasant dalliance. This, however, is not how the General should have spent his morning. He should have been out on the field organising his men for the conflict. Instead, he came lazily and late to meet his enemy. And surely he must have known where the lady's real sympathies lay—her husband, Lord KILMARNOCK, was out there with his men forming a substantial part of Charlie's army.

Had she deliberately diverted Hawley from his proper business? Was it a plot? Did her charm and a whiff of her perfume overpower Hawley's scent for the fight? Nobody knows, but Lord GEORGE MURRAY, the Prince's right-hand man, took the Jacobites through a tough battle to victory, he having had plenty of time to choose the winning part of the field!

After the battle, the Pretender's army rested in the town and took time to re-provision itself before marching north to Culloden. It was at this time another strange incident caused a stir in the town.

A young private of CLANRANALD was up in his lodgings extracting a shot from a musket he had taken from an Englishman. When he had winkled it out, he fired the musket from the window to get rid of the powder. Unfortunately, it had been double-loaded and that second shot killed young GLENGARRY who was standing in a group of officers on the other side of the road.

Everybody knew it was an accident—even Glengarry said so before he died. But the Glengarrys demanded a severe punishment for the culprit or they would leave the Pretender's army.

It is said that in order to preserve unity, Clanranald agreed to deal with their soldier themselves. Without wasting time, they shot him. Even his father, they say, put a bullet in him.

Prince Charles was most upset by the

incident and decreed that the lad be given a burial befitting a hero, in the grave of Sir WILLIAM WALLACE's right-hand man, Sir JOHN GRAHAM, a valiant of the first Battle of Falkirk. Rumour has it, though, that the soldier was buried in a grave *near* the Graham Tomb. Experts say he is certainly *not* in the great man's Tomb.

There is also doubt as to whether that unfortunate soldier really *is* buried in Falkirk. Is it possible that satisfaction for the Glengarrys was more illusion than reality? Was that lad really shot? Or were the vengeful Glengarrys tricked?

WHO
WAS THE
JOKER?

AMONG the many treasures to be seen at
Glamis Castle are a few books from the
Cromwellian period, and these are
printed on very special paper.

It could be said that the Scots
were not over-fond of CHARLES I,
the lad born in Dunfermline,
but they surely had a lot less
liking for OLIVER CROMWELL who
really did knock them about a bit.
Charles, after all, did have one or two
appealing virtues, and when he was beheaded in Whitehall, a ripple of sympathy for
him quivered through the land of his birth.
But, what's the connection between all this
and those Cromwell books?

CHARLES I
[after
VANDYKE]

The books were printed on paper which
must have been the first of its kind to be
called 'foolscap'. In Glamis Castle they tell
the tale of how it came to be so called.

The papermakers, wishing to show
respect to Cromwell—since he was the new
boss—humbly asked him what watermark
he wished to have on the new state paper.

The Protector is supposed to have replied, 'Oh, you'd better go on using the old fool's cap'—meaning the crown of Charles I. The papermakers are said to have taken the instruction literally, and so the watermark turned out to be a Jester's head with a cap and bell! The paper became known as 'foolscap' and this term has endured down through the centuries.

OLIVER CROMWELL

Questions, though, have to be asked. Did the Jester's head really find its way on to the paper because of a misunderstanding? Or was there a Scottish sympathiser who had a hand in the matter? Was he remembering all the pain that Cromwell inflicted on Scotland? Was the Jester's head a deliberate sending-up of the great Oliver? The trick certainly has the flavour of Scottish humour about it.

THE
PICTS'
ELIXIR

ALL over Scotland, stories are told of ancient brews boiled up from the most outlandish ingredients, some of them just too disgusting to be described. One of the less harmful concoctions would be nettle beer, for which no particular properties are claimed.

But, down on the Mull of Galloway, not far from St Medan's Cave, there are the remnants of some Pictish entrenchments called the Double Dykes. These have an association with an ancient, secret brew. And this is where the Picts made, possibly, their last stand against the invading Scots from Ireland.

Now, it is also possible that the reason the Picts had been so successful at holding off the attacks of the superior Scots army for a long time was by imbibing a secret heather brew which set up the partaker with such energy and confidence that no difficulty could stand in his way.

But, it was not just *any*body who could brew up this special heather tipple. Only the Pictish chief and his two sons knew the recipe. And they held on to the secret even when their forces were finally overwhelmed by the Scots.

It was then that a treacherous Druid squealed to the Scots about the chief and his sons being the only ones who knew the formula for the booze that made men super-human. The Scots, having also heard the tales about the Picts' secret liquid weapon, wanted to know more.

The invaders took the chief and his sons prisoner, thinking it would be easy to get the information they wanted. All they had to do was torture it out of them. The brutality was just about to begin when one of the sons cried, 'Throw my father and brother over the cliff on to the rocks and I'll tell you the secret!'

Well, thought the Scots leader, this is even simpler than I thought, so he promptly had the Pictish chief and his other son hurled onto the ragged boulders far below.

Then the surviving son cast himself over the precipice shouting, 'The secret dies!'

That lad knew that the Scots would eventually kill all three of them anyway.

Thus the secret did indeed die with those three brave men. The magic ale has never been supped in Scotland since.

Or, has it … ?

HELLO
SAILOR!

MOST people have surely heard of JOHN
PAUL JONES of Kirkbean—a big shot in the
United States Navy. But, who knows about
TOMMY COCHRAN? Not so many, I guess.

Tom was born at Lanark in 1775, eldest
son of the ninth Earl of DUNDONALD. He
attained the rank of Admiral in the British
Navy and also found time to be a Member
of Parliament.

While attacking the French Navy in the
Basque Roads in 1809, Tom got annoyed at
the lack of support from the man in command, Admiral GAMBIER. Tom complained
and Gambier was court-marshalled, but
acquitted. The incident then boomeranged
on Cochrane and he was discredited! Poor
Tom was thrown out of the Order of the
Bath, accused of dipping into Navy funds,
and given a year in jail, as well as a fine.

After that year, understandably, Tom
headed for pastures new. This amazing
fellow went off to command the Chilean
Navy, and then the Brazilian Navy, before
coming back to Europe to run the Greek

Navy! Meantime, back home, the clouds lifted for Tom. In 1832, he was given a free pardon for the crime he had not committed, and the Establishment put him back into the Order of the Bath. Could all this perhaps have had something to do with his becoming the tenth Earl of Dundonald?

Now, real fame came to Tommy Cochrane when he announced that he had devised a plan—totally secret and known only to him—by which he could destroy any fleet or fortress in the world! The British authorities took him most seriously, even though they had been reluctant to take his advice when he was the first person to urge the Navy to adopt steam power.

So, he was invited to talk to them. What was this secret plan which would win mastery of the world for its possessor?

Inconveniently, Tommy Cochran died in 1860 and took his secret plan with him to the grave. No one has ever had a clue as to what it might have been.

Now, come on, Tom, did you really have a master plan? Or were you just getting a bit of your own back on the British author-ities for the way they had treated you? Are you still laughing your head off in Heaven?

THE
HOUSE OF
SECRETS

SOME older people around the Fort William area still talk about the House of Secrets, standing almost twenty miles north of the town.

Inverlair Lodge is in a picturesque but isolated part of Inverness-shire. It is very old and may have been a farmhouse before it became a shooting lodge for the Victorians.

During World War II, it was taken over by the British Army—but for what purpose? Local folk say it was a centre for British Intelligence, and all types of service people were seen coming and going at all times of day and night. The visitors were not just British—it seems that people from almost every country in Europe did spells of varying lengths at Inverlair.

Once a week, a truckload of Inverlair inhabitants came down to Fort William on an off-duty outing, but no conversation could ever be struck up by the locals with those strangers.

Another rumoured feature of the place was that no beverages of an alcoholic nature were allowed through the portals of that mysterious place!

Stories about Inverlair grew like mushrooms. One tale stated that it was a holding place for British trained agents who, for a variety of reasons, didn't make the grade to full agent status. They had, however, become privy to certain classified information which they could not be allowed to take home with them.

Other people in Fort William said that high-ranking German officers, captured on the various war fronts, were brought to be interrogated at Inverlair. Even the German RUDOLPH HESS, it is alleged, spent some time there after his infamous Eaglesham parachute landing.

Usually, after the passage of years, places like Inverlair offer up the secrets of their war-time undercover operations. But this House of Secrets does not seem to have revealed anything. Why should the cloud of mystery still hang over it? And will the wind of revelation ever blow it away?

WHAT'S
A
DISSY?

A MARVELLOUS restoration has been
made recently of the tiny village of New
Lanark. With the place having lain derelict
and silent for a few decades, it was difficult
to imagine it as it once was—a community,
bursting with life.

DAVID DALE, a prosperous Glasgow
cotton merchant, built his cotton mills there
and at Blantyre, round about the mid 1870s.
Each location was where a convenient bend
in the Clyde allowed the cutting of a lade
to provide water-power

DAVID
DALE

These were not just business
enterprises. Dale was the kind of
Christian who felt he had social
responsibility. He began building
complete communities, with
housing for his mill-workers and
education for their children.

His son-in-law, Welshman
ROBERT OWEN, continued this
mission at New Lanark towards
Utopia, with even greater fervour.
He spread his patriarchal

protection around his New Lanark villagers, taking personal responsibility for their physical and moral welfare. He continued his concern right until the time of his death.

But, as time passed, foreign competition in the cotton trade grew. The New Lanark mills gradually fell silent. People moved away. It is quite remarkable that at least one mill managed to keep going right into the 1930s.

Shortly afterwards the entire village lay empty, the mills stripped of their machinery. The only signs of life about the place were nesting pigeons and spreading weeds.

That was until the recent restoration. Tenements were refurbished to modern standards and people flocked back to enjoy living in that beautiful village. The mills are now a wonderful tourist attraction, telling the fascinating history of New Lanark.

While renewal work was going on in one of the mills, it was noticed that right on the very top floor some interesting graffiti could still be seen. The roof was formed of timber trusses tied together with metal purlins, and the slating laid over these. Along one of those purlins, some words had been scrawled with chalk. Time had faded them but they were still legible—'AGNES DISSIED IAN—JUNE, 1933'. Of course there is no such verb in the English language as 'to dissy', but anyone who lived in earlier times in the West of Scotland would know that the message conveyed the information that a girl called Agnes had been invited out on a date by a boy called Ian. Agnes failed to turn up for the tryst, so Ian got a disappointment—hence this peculiar local verb, 'to dissy'.

But who were Agnes and Ian? Did romance flourish for them later on? Or did they go their separate ways? An answer to the hasty scrawl might make an intriguing story.

WHERE
LIES
FARQUHAR'S
FORTUNE?

IN the Black Isle they still talk about
FARQUHAR MCLENNAN, sometimes known
as 'Farquhar of the Gun'. His life crossed
over from the eighteenth century into the
nineteenth; and if the world at large didn't
know him, Ross-shire certainly did.

He was the most sartorially colourful
tramp ever known in that area. He wore a
hat covered in feathers of many hues and
with added paper decoration. An iron chain
held his hat round his chin. An even heavier
chain around his waist kept his multi-
coloured clothes from flapping about. Also
hanging from that chain were bits of bones,
rags, pieces of metal, pistols (hence his
nickname), and a powder horn of Mexican
origin.

It is said that Farquhar's odd ways dated
from the time that a farmer he was working for clobbered him over the head with a
shovel for some misdemeanour. Poor
Farquhar changed his lifestyle—including
his manner of dress—and took to the road
as a tramp.

He begged for money in villages and at farmhouses, and often he would grace the house he was visiting by praying a long, but surprisingly beautiful, prayer. He would also, in the prayer, draw attention to his small store of worldly goods compared with the large fortunes of others, but stressed that he was not chiding the Deity on this account!

His hobby could be described as very unusual—he loved blowing up stones! That's why he had the powder horn. Local gamekeepers kept him supplied with explosive. Some of his stone chips must still be scattered around some of the old tracks of the Black Isle.

The story goes that he was blowing up stones on the very day he died, but there is no evidence that he actually blew himself up! He did, however, go out with a bang at the age of 84.

He was so well looked after by local people that he never needed to spend any of the money he had gathered over the years. Indeed, he declared he had buried his considerable hoard somewhere in the Black Isle, but it has never been discovered.

Now, there's a mystery ....

WHAT
IF TOM
HAD SAVED
THE KING?

YOU could ask around for weeks on end
and still not find one Scot who had heard of
THOMAS MUIR of Huntershill. Yet, the
story of this remarkable man could make a
fascinating television serial of adventure,
passion and courage.

So, who was he? Born in Glasgow in
1765, Thomas was the offspring of a hop
merchant whose shop was in High Street.
Generations of his father's people had been
farmers in the Kirkintilloch area.

Young Muir was a bright lad and nobody was particularly surprised when he

GLASGOW UNIVERSITY *in the* EIGHTEENTH CENTURY

went to study Law at Glasgow University. But it was there that he began to show traits which didn't fit into the pattern of a conventional, respectable son of a fairly well-to-do, middle class family.

This is what happened. Thomas's favourite professor at Glasgow was outrageously maligned when he exposed some corruption in the college. Thomas spoke out strongly in support of his tutor. This prompted the hierarchy to start a 'freezing-out' campaign against him. He was no longer welcome at that seat of learning.

Edinburgh University, however, was glad to accept him, and there he completed his studies.

Muir then became one of those tiresome nuisances demanding—in an entirely *peaceful* way—serious parliamentary reform and a wider franchise. He and his friends were promoting their cause just as the excesses of the French Revolution were beginning to frighten many people in Britain. Thus, those who perhaps in calmer times might have supported Muir and his group, now backed off.

It was just a matter of time before the rebels faced the grim judge, Lord BRAXFIELD, on charges of sedition. Muir and his friends were banished to Australia's Botany Bay. From that penal colony, Muir escaped to

America, was battered about in other people's conflicts, seriously disabled and then finally exiled in France.

But let's go back a bit—before Muir's fall from grace, he actually went to France. He was concerned about the brutalities which were disfiguring any effort to achieve liberty, equality and fraternity in that hate-racked country. He went there as soon as he heard the masses were about to behead King LOUIS XVI. Such crimes, he was sure, would damn the cause of justice for all.

Muir arrived in Paris on 21st January 1793. The revolutionaries listened to his objections politely. Some were even swayed by his plea that the King should not be executed. But alas, his plea came too late. Louis died that very day.

Imagine if Tom Muir had got there earlier and had more time to drive home his argument? Could the King have been saved. If so, would the whole course of European politics and international relations have been radically changed? And would history now tell a different story?

NO
SUNDAE
ON SUNDAY

THE enormous social problems caused by
heavy drinking since the last century
brought into existence a remarkable army
of Temperance organisations. In Scotland,
they performed miracles in saving families
from utter degradation. For instance, the
Good Templars were responsible for a social
project which became part of the folk history
of Glasgow.

The Good Templars organised Saturday
evening concerts for the whole family in
three different venues, with entertainment
running simultaneously in the three halls.
Top-class variety acts were employed, and
as each entertainer finished his or her act at
one hall, and had taken the applause of the
audience, he or she was whisked by hansom
cab to the second location, and then the
third.

Each show began with the singing of
Psalm 100. Tea and pokes of buns were
given to all. Then the chairman, after the
repast, invited the entire audience to blow
up their empty pokes and, on a signal from

him, a great mass of raised hands, in unison, smacked down on the pokes! The bursting reverberated round the auditorium like thunder! This stopped sporadic bursting during the show! That's why those concerts were called 'The Bursts'.

The shows were spectacularly successful in keeping men out of the pubs on Saturday nights, and drunkenness began to drop dramatically in the city.

Other groups, such as the Band of Hope and the Rechabites, also provided happy diversions and contributed substantially to the control of heavy drinking. But there were other anti-drink associations with more unusual, even aggressive, approaches.

One women's organisation which was particularly belligerent, invited the Kansas pub-smasher, CARRIE NATION, to Glasgow. Her methods were direct. She and her mates just marched right into a pub and smashed up everything in sight!

Now, a situation arose which must have a question mark over it. Carrie invited her Glasgow lady friends to join her in an exercise of pub-plundering. She must have felt utterly let down when not one Glasgow lady took up this attractive offer. Why ever not?

Another odd development came at the height of the battle against the evil drink.

The British Women's Temperance Association suddenly switched its attack from drink to ice-cream! They delivered a petition to the Lord Provost in Glasgow decrying the opening of ice-cream shops on Sundays.

The outcry against Sunday ice-cream spread. Edinburgh, Dundee and Aberdeen joined in. The Provost of Perth spoke of the 'ice-cream pestilence'! He condemned ice-cream shops as 'howffs of enjoyment'.

But what made ice-cream innocent on Saturday, but evil on Sunday? Why this change of tack when drink was still public enemy number one? Odd ... very odd.

ANOTHER
CRAZY
MIXED-UP
STEWART

EARLY in his reign, King JAMES V seems to have been quite a merry monarch with a liberal disposition. Later he changed, and different reasons are given for the change.

One reason, it is said, was the growing opposition he had to contend with from the Douglases. They were plotting his downfall and he was driven to executing quite a few of them for conspiracy.

Second, his first wife, MAGDELEN, had died, and the King was severely affected by his loss. Afterwards he married the formidable French lady, MARY of GUISE, who was destined to arrange some major twists and turns in Scottish history.

Concerning the Douglases, observers at the Court reported that the King's hatred for them grew into an obsession. He had the most fearful nightmares about the Douglas family and would wake up screaming!

At that time, JANET DOUGLAS married the sixth Lord GLAMMIS and thus began her role in one of Scotland's great whodunits.

Four years after her husband's death in

1528, Janet was accused of poisoning him.
The accusers at her trial couldn't really
mount a case against her and she was found
not guilty. But as she was one of those hated
Douglases, something had to be cooked up
to prove that she was an evil person—even
a witch! The lady had not long to wait.

The cooking produced yet another
Douglas conspiracy and Janet was accused,
not only of witchcraft, but of actually
plotting to poison the King! Her second
husband, ARCHIE CAMPBELL, was also
accused. At that sham trial she was found
guilty, this time without even an attempt
by her captors to produce any real evidence.
She was condemned to death by burning.

The penalty was exacted at Edinburgh
Castle in either July or December, 1540.

That beautiful noblewoman is said to
have passed into eternity without the slightest sign of fear. Her husband was still in
the castle, and, attempting to escape, he
fell to his death all the way down the Castle
Rock.

Soon after, there was one of those mind-
boggling little incidents which make daft
footnotes to Scottish history. Some fellow
called ALEXANDER MAKKE was supposed to
have provided the poison which Janet tried
to get down the King's gullet. This poor
man had his ears cut off and was banned

EDINBURGH CASTLE *in the* SIXTEENTH CENTURY

from all Scotland—except, strangely enough, from the then county of Aberdeen.

So, why did the King and his cohorts pick particularly on Janet Douglas? Had she denied favours to somebody? And why was Aberdeenshire keen to admit an earless poison-provider banned from the rest of the country?

THE
CRAIGENTINNY
MARBLES

PERHAPS the Craigentinny (or Craigan-tinnie) Marbles aren't as famous as the Elgin ones, but the tale that hangs around them is as intriguing as any Greek fable.

Actually, this monument in a side street off the Portobello Road in Edinburgh, is the mausoleum of WILLIAM HENRY MILLER, Laird of Craigentinny. His grandfather bought the estate in 1764.

The Millers were seedsmen and nursery-men. They were also devout Quakers. William, however, reached out for a more elevated status in life, eventually becoming a Member of Parliament for Newcastle.

He was also renowned as a collector of eccentric books. He built up a magnificent library of very rare volumes. His dividends from the seed and nursery business had made him a man of considerable wealth.

It was not just his books that were eccentric, however. William was too. This led him to make the most unusual arrange-ments for his own funeral.

His mausoleum was to be an impressive

SCENES *from the* CRAIGENTINNY MARBLES

memorial, in keeping with his station in
life. It turned out to be rather 'over the top'
in more senses than one!

A sum of £20,000 was set aside to fund
the project. William Henry Miller had to
be buried in a pit 40 feet deep, lined with
ashlar stone. His body was to be placed in a
series of lead coffins—covered with a heavy
stone slab. Then a beautifully sculptured
monument was to be raised over the pit.

William Henry died in 1848, but prep-
arations for his burial were already under-
way. Nevertheless, the work took so long,
the funeral had to be delayed for six weeks!

Everything was finally completed to
specification, and sculptor ALF GATLEY had
produced the huge rectangular pile for the
top—the monumental crowning glory!

It took 40 men and four horses to lift
and then lay Mr Miller all the way down to
his 40 feet depth and complete the sealing-
off procedure.

Alf Gatley sculpted the most impressive

Sculpted by ALF GATLEY

panels of biblical subjects, set round the sides and ends of the monument. Scenes such as 'The Overthrow of Pharaoh' and 'The Song of Miriam and Moses' were of such quality that the tomb was thereafter called the 'Craigentinny Marbles'.

Why did William Henry want to be encased so far down into the earth? Edinburgh rumour hinted that he had suffered from some awful physical disability which he was desperate to keep secret. Or did he just want to be well out of the way of the bodysnatchers? Only Mr Miller knew, and he kept his reasons to himself.

THE
PIXIES
OF
PLORA

THE author who was known as the 'Ettrick Shepherd', JAMES HOGG, spent about half of his 65 years in the eighteenth century, and the rest in the nineteenth—so he was close enough to that era when all kinds of stories about odd happenings circulated in Scotland.

He used to relate some of them and have a good laugh. But there was one he told which didn't make him laugh, one which he claimed had been authenticated. It concerned the family of a farm worker in a time long before James Hogg was born.

One fine afternoon, the man, whose name was BROWN, was casting turfs on Plora Farm near the village of Traquair. His little daughter, JANE, was playing around him, making him laugh with her prattle. The job he was doing was the kind that lures the mind into faraway thoughts, detached from the immediate scene. After a

JAMES
HOGG

while, he came out of his absent-minded spell and realised that Jane wasn't prattling any more. He looked all around him and couldn't see her. Shouting her name didn't bring her back into view. Jane had simply disappeared!

Though her dad searched frantically in every field, bush and hedge, and in the woods and by the river, he just could not find her! All the people of the parish joined in the search, but she was nowhere to be found.

Her father reckoned that in the open country around him she couldn't have run fast enough to get out of his sight as he raced round looking for her. Where had she gone?

Distracted, the poor man sought the help of the minister of Innerleithen—a man known for his wisdom. The minister gave instructions to the congregations of the seven churches in the district that they should pray, on the Sabbath, at precisely the same hour.

That Sunday the seven congregations did indeed pray, as one voice, for the safe return of Jane Brown. Subdued, the people drifted home ....

Amazingly, within the hour, the wee lassie was found down by Plora Wood, idly picking the bark from a tree. She was tidy, bright-eyed and she wasn't hungry. Indeed, she was happily singing away to herself. Her skin had a slightly bluish tinge, but that wore away in a few weeks. She was in perfect health and wondered what all the fuss was about!

Jane Brown lived to be a very old lady. Had she been taken away by the pixies, as was mooted at the time? If not, what was the explanation for her vanishing? It's not likely that anybody will ever find out.

THE MYSTERY
OF THE
MISSIONARY'S
SON

THERE have been many writers who have attempted to explain the rather complex personality of the internationally-acclaimed Scottish folk hero, DAVID LIVINGSTONE. None of them has completely succeeded, because David was a man who couldn't really be explained.

Against impossible odds, David became an educated man, a doctor and teacher. His mission was to bring Christianity and social justice to the heathen peoples of the world. His first thoughts were directed to China, but changing circumstances took him to Africa. There, his achievements were breathtaking —apart from converting the Africans to his faith, he formed their languages into written words and grammar, he brought them new medicines, and he also discovered some of the spectacular physical features of the continent such as Lakes Ngama and Nyassa, the Zambesi River and the Victoria Falls. Probably his greatest triumph, however,

DAVID
LIVINGSTONE

was the smashing of the Arab slave trade.

In his time, he became a cult figure. The Africans loved him. He was lionised by the British public on those few occasions when he came back home. Yet, he seems to have been singularly unsuccessful in getting one young lad to join his fan club.

That lad was ROBERT LIVINGSTONE, his first-born child. Robert grew up to be as strong-headed as his Dad. Indeed, they were both as thrawn as mules and the young lad found it increasingly difficult to do as he was told. As the family waggon-trailed across Africa, Robert was forever wandering off into danger.

Sending him back into the care of two maiden aunts in Scotland only made matters worse. They swiftly dispatched him back to Africa, but he hardly had time to get sunburned before he was on his way back to Liverpool. From there, the restless Robert just simply disappeared!

The story goes that he sailed to America when the Civil War was raging, and joined the 3rd New Hampshire Volunteers in the Northern Army. By then he had changed his name to RUPERT VINCENT. Another sidelight to the story claims he was pressganged in the harbour just after arriving and had no choice but to volunteer! Yet another version of the tale tells that he was accused of desertion, then reprieved, and after all that, wounded and taken prisoner.

He died in that Confederate prisoner-of-war camp. His body now lies, it is said, in the National Cemetery at Gettysburg.

His father suffered the remorse of one who felt he had neglected his family. But couldn't he have made a stronger effort to be reconciled with his recalcitrant son?

And was Robert's fate really as the tales describe? There is more to discover about Robert Livingstone, alias Rupert Vincent.

WAS
IT A
SELL-OUT?

IT might be thought that all there is to say about Scotland's great fighting heroes of the past has all been said—especially about Sir WILLIAM WALLACE. But is this true?

A niggling notion concerning his defeat in the first Battle of Falkirk lingers on to irritate reflection on that conflict. It is thought that the Scottish nobles of his time—well, at least *some* of them—considered Wallace to be just not noble enough to be their leader. They found fault with his battle strategy. Sir JOHN STEWART of Bute, for example, argued a lot with the Guardian of Scotland, and threatened to withdraw his men from the Scottish Army. But, on that bitter St Magdalen's Day in July 1298, at Falkirk, Stewart and his men fought valiantly for Sir William. It was a bloody battle, and, ironically, Sir John died in the thick of the fray.

That day, with time on his side, Wallace chose the firm ground and the best position

The GREAT SEAL *of* EDWARD I *of* ENGLAND

for attack and cover. The boggy ground was left for the army of EDWARD I of England.

Sir William arranged his spearmen in tight *schiltroms*, defensive squares, alternating with groups of archers. In this formation, the Scots awaited the charge of the English cavalry.

That cavalry charged indeed! Men and horses ran into those forests of spears and hail of arrows! The effect was horrifying—dozens of men and horses were impaled on spears, or stuck with arrows like pincushions. Another charge from the Englishmen suffered the same fate. It looked as if a Scots victory was in sight.

But then Edward called up his ranks of longbowmen—a massive force. Their arrows fell on the Scots like the heaviest of hail-showers. The Scots recoiled, but tried heroically to hold on.

WALLACE
MONUMENT
at STIRLING

Wallace knew this was the critical time in the battle and he needed to call down his reserve cavalry from the hill-top behind him. He had been uneasy before the battle started, because of the attitude of some of his noble colleagues. However, in the heat of the hour, he put that from his mind.

He sent up the signal and waited to hear

the thunder of his cavalry's hooves. He heard nothing. He turned to look up the hill. It was deserted. His reserves were simply not there ....

The Scots went down to a bitter defeat. Had those nobles he was so depending on, deliberately betrayed him? Had they, including, interestingly, ROBERT the BRUCE, come to some arrangement with Edward to hand him victory on a plate and cause the downfall of Wallace? What's the answer?

Despite the end result of this battle, it took another seven years to get rid of Wallace, that great Scottish Patriot.

DID
THE ONIONS
CAUSE
THE TEARS?

THERE are still many people who remember the ONION JOHNNIES who pedalled their bicycles around Scotland. They had their machines festooned with strings of onions —front and rear—indeed, in such clusters that the bikes could hardly be seen.

These blokes came from Brittany or Northern Spain, usually wearing corduroys and black berets, and with just enough words of English to sell their onions to housewives or shops or restaurants.

Each man built up his own clientele and made regular visits during the season. Customers often put the kettle on for the arrival of an Onion Johnnie.

Near Parkhead Cross in the East End of Glasgow, in the 1930s, there was a small restaurant called 'Dunn's'. It was not just a landmark, it was a legend. In earlier times, patrons claimed they could enjoy a seven course meal for just sevenpence (old money). They added that the meal consisted of seven penny bowls of soup, a soup which was considered the food of the gods!

A lady called MADGE was the cook in the 1930s and she bought her onions from a Johnnie whom the Parkhead folk called PIERRE. Nobody knew his proper name, nor whether he was French or Spanish. Pierre was Madge's regular. She would buy onions from nobody else. They did business for years together.

Then one day, when Madge was slicing one of Pierre's onions, her knife caught on something rather hard. Imagine her shock and surprise when, as she separated the halves, she found a gold ring right at the centre of the onion!

She was speechless for a while, and, some hours later, she received confirmation hat the ring was gold. It was meant to be worn by a man. The band was thick, and had the letters 'Z.E.B.A.' engraved on its inner surface. Somebody had apparently carefully removed the core of the onion, squeezed the ring into the centre, and replaced the core so that nobody could see any evidence of the surgery!

Madge couldn't bring herself to use that onion! What excitement this incident caused! Patrons and staff could hardly wait for Pierre's next visit to hear if he had an explanation.

The following week, Pierre came back. Madge could never have been prepared for

what happened. She showed her Onion
Johnnie the onion and the ring. He gave an
anguished cry, burst into tears, grabbed the
ring and ran from the shop followed by
Madge and company. He then tossed the
ring through the grating of a drain, jumped
on his bike and sped off! The ring was lost
forever.

Pierre never ever returned to explain his
sorrow ....

WHAT
CHANGED
THE CATTLE'S
COLOUR?

IMAGINE a great fan of roads radiating northwards from Stirling Plain and the Falkirk Tryst—muddy or dusty roads, lined with droves of Highland cattle ambling down the trails, converging on the markets. During a season, thousands of beasts would come from Helmsdale, Strathnaver, Easter Ross, the Uists and Skye. What a sight it would have been from a helicopter!

It seems that cattle were moved about Scotland in this way for some eight hundred years, well into the last century. There would have been little chance of pulling a trailer-caravan past them!

Much of this great tradition and the handling techniques were transported to the American West. Ranch managers and trail bosses were mostly Scots who learned their skills on those Highland roads. They rubbed saddles with such notable characters as BUFFALO BILL CODY and WILD BILL HICKOK.

Highland cattle have now become a prominent feature of the Scottish tourist industry. Many foreign visitors just love those great, shaggy, brown cuddlesome creatures who are so adorable on calendars.

Now here's a mystery—references in the records and accounts concerning Highland cattle during those past centuries, invariably describe them as black. This is not because they got muddy or dusty on the journeys to the markets. They really *were* black.

One writer describing the breed said that these magnificent creatures with shiny black coats and green-tinted horns were the most *durable* of species. So, whatever happened to them?

If you look at artists' pictures of Highland cattle, say from about the middle of the last century, the beasts are all of the brown, cuddly variety. Why did the black cattle not survive?

Answers on a postcard ....

A MYSTERIOUS TWIST IN THE TWEED

IT would be reasonable to deduce that, since bale after bale of tweed cloth was made for donkey's years along the banks of the River Tweed, the cloth had been named after the river. Alas, the deduction in fact would be wrong. Pursuit of the name source leads the enquirer into certain technicalities.

Two hundred years ago, a type of cloth was woven in Scotland, and other places too, which was formed by the *weft* threads crossing over the *warp* on every third or fourth pass of the shuttle. This cloth was called 'tweel' in Scotland and 'twill' in England.

The London merchants of the early years of last century bought their fabrics extensively in Scotland. They appreciated the good quality of Scotland's cloth. Mills in the area around the River Tweed did a roaring trade for years. The rate at which orders came flowing in could be quite hectic.

A story persists that, about 1830, a clerk in one of the Borders mills was rushed off his feet one day, and as he raced against time, the poor man's handwriting began to deteriorate. On one despatch note, he intended to write 'tweel', but his scribble looked more like 'tweed'. When the delivery reached London, some clerk there read the despatch note and forever after described the cloth as 'tweed'. Others picked up the word and it spread around London and over the whole country—and so, 'tweel' became 'tweed'.

This tale is seriously undermined by the fact that the historic despatch note has vanished, and because for years after the alleged coining of the name 'tweed', many people claimed to have been related to that Borders clerk whose illegible scrawl started the whole daft business.

But, it must be asked, surely experienced textile people down in London would have known the words 'tweel' and 'twill' and would never have misread even a scribbled 'tweel'—*or* invented a new word to take its place!

Then there are those who say maybe another Scots word, 'tweedle', got into the act—although 'tweedle' and 'tweel' referred to linen, not wool.

It is all so confusing!

So, how did 'tweed' get its name? It's anybody's guess ....

WHO
TOOK
THE
MONEY?

FOR generations, workers from Parkhead and Bridgeton in the East End of Glasgow used the pathway along the north bank of the Clyde to reach the mills at Tollcross and Carmyle. That was until the early 1820s when TAM HARVEY, a distiller, bought the Westthorn estate which spread down from the London Road to that north bank.

Tam decided to take his full measure of land and he built a wall right to the water's

HARVEY'S DYKE

edge, thus cutting off the workers' right-of-way. This rather displeased the workers, so they asked Tam politely to take his wall down. He refused. Leading figures in the community requested that he removed it, but he defied all appeals.

So, on Saturday 21st July 1822, a throng of local people demolished the wall with picks and crowbars. Tam called the Ennis-killen Dragoons who happened to be in the city. They promptly rode out and arrested six ringleaders who were jailed.

A wave of sympathy for the wronged workforce swept the country. A fund was established and money poured in. This was used to fight the legal battle against Harvey to win back the right-of-way and the case was finally settled in the House of Lords in favour of the millworkers! It was a triumph for civil rights!

Special medals were struck and awarded to the six men who had been in prison. These men also became members of a trust to administer the cash left over after legal costs had been paid. So they decided to put it all into a bank account.

Some time later, one of the men, ADAM FERRIE, emigrated to Canada, where he prospered and eventually became a senator in the Canadian parliament. Twenty years on, he made his first return trip to Glasgow.

Within a day or so, he was seeking out his old mates. It soon became clear that they were all dead. Adam's next enquiry was at the bank where the cash had been deposited. The manager there could find no record of the account. Many other banks around the city gave the same answer. No trace of the Harvey's Dyke money could be located.

It makes you wonder if one or more of Adam's pals dipped into the cash-box? Or could there be some other explanation?

THE
MYSTERY
OF THE
UNPAID BILL

IT was merely by chance that the brothers, JOHN and CHARLES WOOD, decided to sail their wee boat from Port Glasgow over the Firth of Clyde to Helensburgh, to visit the baths in that elegant town. It was a fine summer's day in 1811. The brothers had just inherited a shipyard from their father.

The baths were managed by one HENRY BELL and his wife. Henry, at one time, had been the Provost of Helensburgh. He was a self-educated man. While ideas buzzed round in his head like bees round a jam-pot, the supreme notion that filled most of his waking hours was the building of a boat that would not depend on wind and a sail to get along, but would be powered by steam! And so, fortune favoured Henry that lovely day. The Wood brothers were just the kind of people he needed to meet.

After the Woods had enjoyed the pleasures of the ablutions, they relaxed in conversation with Henry. He explained his idea. The brothers were impressed. Henry wanted a steamer 40 feet long, 12 feet across the beam and powered by a three-horsepower steam engine. He had it in mind to call the creation 'Comet', because that very year a comet had caused a sensation by flying over Scotland. The brothers agreed to build Henry's boat.

There was much shuttling between Port Glasgow and Helensburgh by Bell and the Woods over many months before Henry's order for the craft was finally in the hands of the shipbuilders. The document did not detail Henry's requirements for his Comet, but indicated what he would pay and when he would pay it. It was in his own hand-writing—with appalling spelling! It read:

'Helensburgh Baths, 27th January, 1813. Three months after date I Promas to pay Messrs John Wood & Co., the sum of one hundred pounds sterling for valaw. Henry Bell, dated 30th January, 1813.'

An extraordinary piece of paper. The 'Comet', of course, sailed into history as the first steampowered vessel to ply open waters in Britain.

But the mystery of the project is that Henry Bell never ever paid that bill. And, even more strangely, the Wood Brothers never pressed him for the payment. And nobody knows why ....

A
FAR-TRAVELLED
BOOK

ONE of the most northerly castles on the Scottish mainland stands between Nairn and Forres. It is called Brodie Castle. Like so many castles in Scotland, Brodie has a history with potential for a gripping TV serial—the BRODIE family have some great tales to tell, often shrouded in mystery.

For instance, in one of the turrets there was a shoogly old staircase which was removed last century. Behind it, the workmen discovered the skeleton of a young child. The mysterious circumstances of how it got there have never been solved.

Even more intriguing is the mystery of the Pontifical. It still baffles those who know all about Pontificals. Pontificals, by the way, were special books of service used in the Roman Catholic Church in the eighth to tenth centuries, but used only by bishops.

Let me explain—a few decades ago, Mrs HELEN BRODIE was searching in the old stables where furniture from past ages was stored. She had three chairs in the castle and knew there had been a set of four. Just imagine the scene—old tables, chairs and sideboards laced with cobwebs … and piles of tatty old books.

Mrs Brodie said that she found the books in question behind a pigeon's nest. There were five volumes of atlases from the seventeenth century—but also a huge religious tome. This turned out to be a Pontifical.

The value of this particular example was not immediately realised. Then the book was shown to the Revd GEORGE SESSFORD who recognised it as a rare volume indeed!

The National Library in Edinburgh identified it as an English tenth century Pontifical—of which only six other copies were known to exist. So this was a major discovery—indeed the find of the century!

The Brodie Pontifical is now in the British Museum. And the experts have searched for clues and studied records without uncovering even a hint of how this precious tome found its way into a castle in the far north of Scotland. A Pontifical is the kind of treasure a bishop should never let out of his sight!

Brodie Castle holds on to its secrets ….

WHO
KILLED
DRUMMOND'S
DAUGHTERS?

LOVE has this inconvenient habit of
drawing men and women into relationships
which don't fit into the plans of the powerful people who hold sway over the lives of
the lovers. The outcome is often sad—even
tragic. You only have to think of ROMEO
and JULIET.

Three blue stone grave slabs lie in a
central position on the floor of the choir of
Dunblane Cathedral, and they are there
because of just such a relationship. The
stones are to the memory of MARGARET
DRUMMOND and her twin sisters, SYBILLA

DUNBLANE CATHEDRAL

and EUPHEMIA. They were the daughters of JOHN, the first Lord DRUMMOND.

There was widespread gossip towards the end of the fifteenth century about Margaret being the mistress of JAMES IV. Indeed, some observers claimed that they had been secretly married.

James apparently made no attempt to quell the gossip. Such was his attraction to the lady that he lavished gifts of land and treasures on her and her family.

Other noble families were clearly unchuffed about the Drummonds becoming the King's favourite indulgence. Tensions grew and something had to give.

The politics of the Scottish Lords at that time were deeply devoted (was it not always so?) to securing the safest bonds they could with the English. And the English took a favourable view of the suggestion from the Scots that both countries would benefit from the marriage of James IV to Princess MARGARET of England. The continuing liaison between the King and Margaret Drummond was an unacceptable nuisance to them. It had to be dissolved—one way or another.

The lords' wish was fulfilled on a day in 1501. Margaret, with her sisters, took breakfast that morning at Drummond Castle. Within a short time, all three had died in agony. The ladies appeared to have been poisoned.

The bodies of the three sisters were taken from Drummond Castle with indecent haste and very quickly buried where they lie to this day. The Dean of the Cathedral at that time was their uncle, WALTER DRUMMOND. He officiated at the interment.

James was devastated. But the iron will of the Scottish Lords prevailed and he did indeed marry Margaret of England two years later. However, he arranged for two priests to be paid five pounds a quarter to say daily mass for his beloved Margaret. This continued until his death at the Battle of Flodden—perhaps a lingering grief for Margaret made James lead his men into that battle instead of commanding from behind as most leaders did ....

Why was no examination carried out to establish what precisely had killed the Drummond girls? Was their uncle perhaps involved in this heinous crime? If not, who really poisoned the sisters? Many questions —but no answers.

COUNT
THE
GUISERS!

HALLOWE'EN 1949—HARRY and JANE, who married just after the War, had set up house in a room-and-kitchen in a tenement on the South Side of Glasgow.

On that 31st October, Jane had left Harry listening to the wireless while she went off to a Hallowe'en soirée at the kirk hall.

She got back about ten o'clock and asked Harry if he had been bothered much by the guisers. He said one or two strange weans had come to the door, but his main visitors had been the usual gang of boys and girls from the tenement—the neighbours' children. They had done their party-pieces—some sublime, some excruciating—for nuts, apples and sweets.

He remembered that the two McLauchlins were there ... the McLeod twins ... wee John Semple ... and Mary Reeves. Oh, and there had been another wee laddie, fair-haired, about eleven years old—must be new to the street. Harry certainly didn't know him. The lad had said that his name was Robin Wells. So that was seven weans in all ....

Next morning, Jane met MARY REEVES on her way to school.

Jane said, 'Some crowd of your lot up in our house last night, eh? Who was that new boy with you? Wells? Robin Wells?'

Mary said, 'Robin *who*? No. It was just me and the McLaughlins and the McLeods and wee Semple .... '

Jane's mother was listening to them. She had lived in that tenement since the 1920s. When she heard her daughter's story, she suddenly said, 'Oh, my goodness! Wells ... the family who lived on the top flat. They moved away to Coventry ... yes ... a few months before the War broke out in 1939. The man's work took them there.

'Aye, Robin ... he was a big lad for his age. Must've been ten when they left here. ... They were down in Coventry that night when the German planes came over. No ... that's impossible. Harry must've got the name wrong. Must have been somebody else.'

So did Harry make a mistake? Was one of the children guising that night a fair-haired laddie called, by sheer coincidence, Robin Wells?

Harry never talks about that Hallowe'en now ....

DOOM
ON
DOON HILL

DOON Hill is not particularly eye-catching.
It is just one of the group of hills huddling
round behind the coast town of
Dunbar. There is nothing about
Doon Hill which suggests it may
have been the scene of one of
Scotland's most dreadful cal-
amities. But it certainly was.

High on that hill, on the
morning of 2nd September 1650,
General DAVID LESLIE had assem-
bled his Scottish Army of the Covenant.

General
DAVID
LESLIE

Down on a peninsula near the harbour, the
invading army of OLIVER CROMWELL was
crammed into a wee space, which was all
the ground that Cromwell held in Scotland
at that time. He was most uncomfortable.
His Englishmen were in poor spirits, and
he was remembering how, just five years
back, Leslie had routed the army of the
Marquess of MONTROSE at Philiphaugh,
near Selkirk. So, Cromwell knew Leslie was
among the most respected military men of
Europe.

It was also less than encouraging to be aware that the Scots outnumbered the English by almost two to one! It seemed that David Leslie had the nap hand to defeat the oncoming English Army.

The Scots had their tails up and seemed to be waiting for Cromwell's forces to try a full frontal move or a flanking manoeuvre. The English Army stood alert ... ready for action. What happened then defies explanation! Cromwell could hardly believe his eyes—or his luck!

The Scots suddenly came down the hill in a ragged, undisciplined, unprofessional rush—a rabble running wild. Oliver's men picked off the scrabbling Scots with ease. It was incomprehensible to him that the master military tactician, Leslie, could have orchestrated this shambles. Three thousand Scots died that day—Leslie gifted Cromwell almost free passage through Scotland.

But, why did it happen? What caused this renowned soldier to commit the act of a madman? Had he been pressured by the zealous, perhaps *over*-zealous, Covenanting ministers in his entourage, their persistent urging forcing him into this foolhardy action? Or was that great military mind overtaken by some strange malady laying siege to his senses ... ?

WHAT'S IN A NAME?

THE bright full moons of the spring of 1941 illuminated the targets when the German *Luftwaffe* concentrated its destructive attention on the West of Scotland. Clydebank, Greenock, Dumbarton and Glasgow took the brunt.

In the first week of May, the bombers were over Greenock and Dumbarton. In Greenock, people spoke of seeing rivers of burning sugar and whisky running down towards the Clyde from the bombed distillery and sugar refinery.

On one particular night, the residents of the little village of Cardross, four miles from Dumbarton on the Helensburgh road, listened to that heart-chilling throbbing from the aircraft passing overhead. They watched in awe as the inferno grew on both sides of the Firth in the distance. Dumbarton and Greenock, with their shipbuilding yards and factories making munitions and aircraft parts, were what the Germans called 'legitimate' targets. Cardross, however, had no such war-support facility.

Suddenly, the War came crashing into that village with a scatter of incendiary bombs. Firefighters were doing their best to control the blaze in the parish church when a high-explosive bomb shattered the building. The bare walls of what remained of the kirk have been left as a memorial.

Why was Cardross bombed? There was nothing for the Germans here. Was it a random bombing—maybe crews ditching the last of their loads before flying home?

It was hardly general knowledge during the War that, for safety and security reasons, ammunition dumps were spread all over the remote areas of the country—usually in underground stores. Only after the War was this arrangement made known to the public. One of those dumps was located near the Lake of Menteith, well away from the bombers' target areas. But a glance at the ordnance survey map reveals there is a place, also near the Lake, called Cardross—yes, another one—and it has now been revealed as the exact location of that ammunition dump!

Did the Germans know there was a dump at this Cardross? Did they assume there was only one 'Cardross' and bomb the undefended Clydeside village of the same name? Or were they dropping bombs at random? No answer has been given.

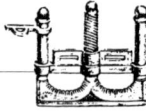

WHAT BECAME OF MRS MILLS?

SURELY one of the most remarkable women in Scottish history was the Countess of NITHSDALE, wife of the fifth Earl. She was staying at Traquair House near Peebles when the shocking news came through that the 1715 Jacobite Rebellion had collapsed. Her husband had been captured and was on his way to imprisonment in London.

Many a wife in those days would have sat there sobbing—but not this lady. She determined either to cajole the enemy, GEORGE I, into pardoning her man, or, as a last resort, organise his escape from jail.

So the Countess headed for London in the dead of winter. Although her stage-coach got stuck in the snow somewhere near York, she and her Welsh servant, CECILIA EVANS, carried onwards on horse-back with the snow up to the stirrups!

They finally made it to London, but what a task the Countess had set herself! Getting her message across to the King must have been difficult enough—he was German and hardly spoke a word of

English! Whatever he understood of her plea, he nevertheless rejected it.

Thus she began on Plan B. Her project was delayed when she was laid low by severe illness, but she took the opportunity of enforced bed-rest to plan her next move. As soon as she was able to stand upright again, she was ready to begin.

The Countess was given permission to visit her husband in his cell and she, with Cecilia, made regular visits. One day, the Countess came to see her husband, not just with Cecilia, but also with a new friend—a well-built lady called Mrs MILLS. Under their voluminous clothing, the ladies had smuggled in another full set of women's apparel. At the end of the visit, the guards saw the three ladies emerge from the Earl's cell. They did not notice that the one of much the same build as Mrs Mills was not in fact Mrs Mills!

The Earl was whisked off immediately to France. The Countess, pretending to have forgotten something, returned to the cell to ensure a substantial delay before any guard noticed that Mrs Mills, now sitting in the cell, was not of male nobility. This allowed more time for the Earl to be well on his way to freedom.

No account of this tale explains the subsequent fate of 'Mrs Mills' ....

WHAT DID
THE QUEEN
PROMISE
THE REGENT?

THE dice of Fate fell awkwardly for the
first and second Earls of MORAY. It is easy
to get the two mixed up. The first was the
illegitimate son of JAMES V. The second was
the son-in-law of the first and the man
known as the 'Bonie Earl o' MORAY' who
was done to death by the 'heavies' of King
JAMES VI.

King James VI was annoyed that his
Queen had taken a real shine to the Bonie
Earl. On a dark night, the Earl's house at
Donibristle was set on fire by James's thugs.

Moray might have escaped by a back
way, but his silk scarf was set alight by
sparks from the burning house, making
him an easy target for a murdering sword.

O, lang may his Lady
Look ower the Castle Doune,
Ere she see the Earl o' Moray
Cam soondin through the toon.

Long before the crime at Donibristle,
the *first* Earl of Moray, the father-in-law,

had often displayed his political talents. He
was the first Regent after the enforced abdi-
cation of MARY Queen of Scots.
The Earl was her half-brother.
And Mary's son, that same
murdering James VI, did not
yet have a head big enough
to fit the crown. He was just
a wean.

Mary, of course, escaped
from her captivity in Loch Leven
Castle, attempted to defeat the Regent's
forces at Langside, failed, and fled south to
England where the fickle Queen ELIZABETH
imprisoned her for a very long time before
having her beheaded.

JAMES
STEWART,
EARL *of*
MORAY

However, in the early years of Mary's
English captivity, Regent Moray, for quite
a while, played all the correct moves in his
political chess game with Queen Bess. He
really impressed her. He made it clear that
her interests and security were dear to his
heart and it seemed that she believed him.

But he really took her breath away by
suggesting that, with the French and the
Spanish plotting to her detriment, the
Reformed Faith could be in danger—and
Catholic Mary's presence in England added
to the danger! Elizabeth should return
Mary to his safe-keeping in Scotland. If she
did so, Moray said he would send the Earl

of Northumberland, whom he was holding, back to Queen Elizabeth.

Just before Elizabeth's messengers arrived in Scotland with her reply to the Regent's suggestion, JAMES HAMILTON of Bothwellhaugh fired the fateful shot which mortally wounded the Regent in a Linlithgow street on 21st January 1570.

Elizabeth immediately recalled her messengers and the message has never been revealed. What had her answer been? And might it have changed the course of Scottish history ... especially for the ill-fated Mary Queen of Scots?

THE MYSTERY OF THE STONE

EVER since EDWARD I stole the Stone of Destiny from Scone in 1296, questions and arguments have been lobbed in all directions concerning its origins and ultimate fate. The questions and arguments multiplied rapidly after the removal of the Stone from Westminster Abbey in 1950 and even more so after its subsequent return to Westminster. The final word on the truth of the matter is now said to have been expressed. But, has it?

Let the story of the Stone be picked up again from the days when it first rested in the Abbey of Scone, a sanctuary long since vanished.

The Coronation Stone of the Kings of Alba was, according to tradition, used by JACOB, son of ABRAHAM, as a pillow at Bethel. What a pillow! Twenty-six inches long, sixteen inches broad and ten-and-a-half inches deep, that red sandstone block was hardly likely to

The CORONATION CHAIR, WESTMINSTER ABBEY, *containing the* STONE *of* DESTINY

induce sleep—unless it was by hard contact!

Jewish tradition has it that the Stone became the pedestal of the Ark of the Covenant in the Temple. Through a whole series of remarkable circumstances, it was brought via Egypt, Spain and Ireland, to rest in the Abbey of Scone. And there it lay until that thief Edward I carried it off to Westminster Abbey.

But, did he really?

There is a story about a farm lad who, sometime around the late eighteenth or early nineteenth century, was caught in a sudden storm near his farm at Dunsinnan. Racing for shelter, he bumped into a pal also seeking refuge.

What a surprise for them when they discovered that the monsoon-like rain had caused the land to slip down a hillside. The slide revealed an opening which had not been there before. They crawled in and, when their eyes became accustomed to the gloom, they noticed a rectangular stone supported on four smaller stones. Since there seemed to be no value in those lumps of masonry, the boys went home when the storm abated and forgot all about their cave experience.

Some years later, the lad from the Dunsinnan farm heard the story of two monks of Scone who were alarmed when word came to them that King Edward was heading there and would likely pinch the Stone. They went down to the Annety Burn and selected a bit of stone which resembled the Stone, put the substitute in the Abbey and hid the real Stone in a small hillside cave near Dunsinnan.

That farm lad, older and wiser, rushed back to the hillside where he had sheltered from the storm all those years before. Alas, more recently, another landslide had obliterated the small cave.

The question continues to niggle away in some minds—does the true Stone of Destiny remain to this day under a hill near Dunsinnan?

WHAT
CAUSED
SCOTLAND'S
METEOROLOGICAL
ABERRATION?

THE last decade of the seventeenth century into the eighteenth, saw Fate kicking Scotland so regularly in the teeth that the country must have been down to gnashing its gums! The massacre at Glencoe in 1692 left a deep scar on the Scottish folk memory, but the killings on that ghastly February night were in small proportion to the hundreds, even thousands, of deaths inflicted on the Scots population by the strange, cruel weather of the seven long years from 1696.

WILLIAM III, 'King BILLY', had been on the throne for five years when the seasons in Scotland went daft! The sun seldom shone, it was mostly cold and barren, cattle lost

weight and died, crops failed, and flies and clegs vanished. Even the invincible Scottish midge was vanquished! Sheep were being sheared in desperation as late as November and December. The author FLETCHER of SALTOUN wrote in 1698 of the thousands who would die in the coming years for want of bread. His forecast came bitterly true. Scots thereafter referred to that grim time as 'King William's Years'.

Through all of this, Scotland was also agonising over the appalling disaster of Darien, the scheme of colonisation on the Isthmus of Panama. It was an open secret that neither England nor Spain were praying for the success of the Scottish project. Indeed, when disease began to kill off the colonists like flies and their whole operation became impossible, the English and the Spaniards did not raise one finger to help.

There are tales of how some Scots ships, carrying the remnants of the pioneer group, left Darien with the vain hope of reaching home. Their fate remains unknown ....

The view was widespread that all these afflictions fell upon the Scots as punishment for their sins. Support for this has decreased over the years. But, the question remains— what brought about Scotland's weather ailments? Is there a scientific explanation or were they linked to the man-made kind?

THE
MYSTERY
OF
RICHARD II

WHAT a shabby lot of Royalty! Really, that's a fitting description for the bunch Scotland suffered from in the back end of the fourteenth century.

King ROBERT III, for example, was a bit of a wimp. Indeed, he was so inept at running the affairs of state that the nobles of the realm decreed that he must give up the job of monarch and let his son, the Duke of ROTHESAY, take over.

RICHARD II [*from* WESTMINSTER ABBEY]

All the while, hovering over the political manoeuvres, was the King's brother, the Duke of ALBANY. He was a nasty piece of work, the man responsible for the murder of his own nephew, the above mentioned Duke of Rothesay, in Falkland Palace.

Mystery surrounds this murder, but it was said that the Duke was starved to

death. He, having said this, was every bit
as nasty his uncle.

About that time, RICHARD II of England
was also being given his redundancy notice.
His cousin, HENRY of Hereford, called
himself HENRY IV and took the throne.

King Richard was then alleged to have
been murdered while being held prisoner
in Pontefract Castle. But was he?

You see, Henry IV was getting a bit
peeved at the Scots who constantly nibbled
away at his borders. At least, that's the up-
front story given as the reason why Henry
IV led his army into Scotland (the last
English king to do so), supposedly to sort
out those obstreperous natives.

But, rather strangely, the expedition
was shy about the usual looting and
pillaging. Unlike previous English visitors,
Henry did not ransack a single Scottish
village or abbey. All he did was set siege to
Edinburgh Castle with yon same Duke of
Rothesay (yes, son of Robert III) inside it.
(This was some time before the Duke went
on his enforced slimming course at Falkland Palace.)

Henry made no attempt to attack
Edinburgh Castle, and after a few weeks
stay, he packed up and went home. The
whole expedition appeared quite odd.

Another story claims that Henry's true

mission was to collect his cousin Richard who had not in fact been murdered, but had escaped from Pontefract Castle and fled to Scotland. For, all this time, down in Yorkshire (the tale continues) the body of a man called MAUDELAIN had been passed off as that of Richard.

STIRLING CASTLE

Henry, however, withdrew from Scotland without his regal relative. Richard (the same deposed Richard II of England!) is supposed to have been kept under a shroud of secrecy at Stirling Castle until he died and then he was buried there with all the trappings of majesty denied to him in his own land.

Was Richard really a political refugee? Does his body lie in Stirling Castle? Or did he really face death down south in Pontefract Castle at the murderous hands of his cousin?

DID SOMEBODY PAY THE IRISHMAN?

FROM Dublin's fair city, there came to Inverness in 1849 one TOM MULOCK. This extraordinary Irishman stayed there for 18 months as editor of the Inverness *Advertiser* creating the slogan for the newspaper, 'Justice for Scotland!'

If Tom's career didn't exactly sparkle, it certainly flashed. He had tried his hand at Law and then lectured on Literature somewhere in the English Midlands. Tiring of that, the restless Irishman became a Baptist minister. At his church in Stoke he had a set of pews railed off from the rest and that segregated section was reserved for those members of his congregation whom Tom deemed to be the most godly!

Soon, he shot off in another direction—this time as a crusading journalist. But making the Prince Consort a target for criticism did not win him popularity. A change of location was needed.

On the Inverness *Advertiser*, Tom took up the cause of the poor souls being evicted off their land for the sake of sheep during the notorious Clearances. This was at a time when other Highland newspapers were soft-pedalling on the issue. Mulock travelled all over the Highlands and Islands collecting evidence on what he considered to be a 'social atrocity'.

In a series of open letters, he concentrated on the clearances at Kildonan and Strathnaver. His strongest invective was directed at the second Duke of SUTHERLAND. Tom claimed at one point that imposing exorbitant rents was just one of the Duke's devices to oust the crofters.

However, to the amazement of readers, the Irishman suddenly began to back-track on his accusations! Rumour also had it that he had *apologised* to the Duke! Shortly afterwards, Tom vanished from Inverness. Most locals thought the Duke had bought him off. Others wondered if Sutherland had dug up some grimy piece of Tom's past ....

The crusader then surfaced in Paris, now working as a newspaper hack to NAPOLEON III. He became the flavour of the month—but not for much longer than a month!

Without charges being specified, Tom was ordered to leave France immediately or go directly to jail. Thus, once again, Tom flashed out of sight. And the mystery of why Tom's bright glow was swiftly switched off in Inverness and Paris remains unsolved.

ELEPHANT
AND
CASTLE

WHY should an elephant have featured on the coat-of-arms of a medieval Scottish burgh? And why should the elephant have been carrying a castle on its back?

Right up until it lost its burgh status because of the rearrangement of local government, Dumbarton had a coat-of-arms like the one described above. The device is now in abeyance, but the town still keeps a tight grip on its jumbo and fort in case they could be proudly displayed again!

The coat-of-arms is certainly old. It was found in a document dated 1357. But how did the elephant get there? Was it just that people have always been fond of elephants? Didn't everybody sigh, '*Aaaah* …' when Nellie the elephant said goodbye to the circus?

Or, since Dumbarton's motto is *Fortitude et Fidelitas*, and elephants *do* have staying-power and are known to be loyal creatures, was that the reason for Dumbarton giving an elephant this supreme position of honour? Well, wait a minute—a glance around Britain reveals that many places proudly display the elephant-and-castle device. So why did Dumbarton follow the herd?

It has been suggested that, from a particular viewpoint down by the Clyde shore, an observer can easily imagine the shape of Dumbarton Rock to be like an elephant. And the castle is seen to be firmly fixed on the elephant's back.

Another theory is that Dumbuck Hill, just outside the town, used to look like an elephant until quarrying operations slashed it down to the height of a mole heap.

And there is another odd connection. Master Gunner ROMEO DRYSDALE, from Dumbarton, settled in London with his family after his army career. His son opened a pub and what did he called it? Guess?— 'The Elephant and Castle'! It held such a commanding position at the junction of several main roads, that the whole district became know as Elephant and Castle. How many in that famous London location know that their borough is called after the coat-of-arms of Dumbarton? Not many.

But none of the foregoing, interesting as it may be, pins down the truth about the origins of the Dumbarton elephant with a castle for a saddle.

THE
LOVE THAT
LIVED ON

'LENNOXLOVE'—there's a warm, bright
name for a house. It slips easily off the
tongue. Lennoxlove House in Haddington
was once called 'Lethington', a name that
seems more abrasive. The reason for the
change of name is part of Scottish history.
But the last Duke of LENNOX was never to
know that his name would be linked by
love to the great house in Haddington.

FRANCES STEWART, born in 1647,
daughter of the first Lord BLANTYRE, grew
up to be one of Scotland's most celebrated
beauties. She was hardly introduced into
Court circles when she was immediately
chosen as Maid of Honour to CATHERINE,
wife of CHARLES II.

Soon after her appointment, Frances
found that Charles himself was beginning
to take a proprietorial interest in her, so the
young lady dodged clear of him every time
he made a play for her. And to emphasise
her determination not to become the monarch's mistress, she married her true love,
the Duke of Lennox.

Charles was furious! Frances, of course, went right out of favour at Court. She was shunned. And, as if to spite her, the King sent her husband off as ambassador to Denmark.

Sadly, within weeks of the Duke's arrival in Copenhagen, his beautiful wife received devastating news. The story goes that he had been attending a party aboard a ship in the harbour and had accidentally slipped into the water, either from the quayside or from a gang-plank, and he had drowned. Since the Duke was athletic and of a canny disposition, the alleged circumstances of his death were regarded as somewhat unlikely.

Was he pushed? Drugged? Dispatched at the behest of the king? Or was it really an accident? No one really knows.

Frances was invited back to Court, but on a strictly platonic relationship with the King. He did, however, insist that she should be the model for the figure of Britannia which featured on British coinage for centuries. Ironically, soon after, she contracted smallpox which left her disfigured, but right to her death in 1703, her beauty still shone through ....

Her will directed that Lethington House was to be purchased in her name, and that it had to be re-named Lennoxlove, in memory of the real love of her life ....

THE MAN
WITH THE
GOTHIC
MIND

QUITE a flutter of excitement rippled through Edinburgh society in 1832, when the city fathers announced that a grand monument would be raised to the memory of the recently-deceased Sir WALTER SCOTT.

It would be given a prime site on Princes Street and the design would be the winning entry of a competition for which leading artists and architects would be invited to enter. However, it was also to be considered an open competition and anyone who fancied he or she could design a suitable monument, would be allowed to join in.

It was stipulated that the winning design had to be one of 'Gothic purity'.

There was a respectable response from artists and artisans, and after much humming and hawing, the Edinburgh heid yins were ready to make a preliminary selection. But then they had second thoughts—they decided that none of the designs was good enough, and so they rejected all of the entries and set the competition all over again.

It had been noted that the design which

had taken third place in that first round was submitted by one JOHN MORVO. The name seemed oddly familiar and somebody mentioned that a mason at Melrose Abbey back in the fourteenth century had been called John Morvo.

When the result of the second competition was announced, John Morvo's design was given first place. That is the one which can be found in Princes Street to this day.

Now, about the designer. 'John Morvo' turned out to be the pseudonym of a joiner and self-taught draughtsman called GEORGE MEIKLE KEMP.

George was born at Moorfoot Farm in Midlothian and brought up near Carlops. His favourite diversion was to browse around Roslyn Chapel, fascinated by the sculpture of the place.

The priggish Edinburgh authorities, however, were a bit shocked to find that their winner was just a lowly tradesman, but they stuck with George and the work proceeded in Princes Street.

As the monument began to take shape, the criticisms also began to swirl around it. Many accused George of having copied from other buildings. He was bitterly upset by the sneering comments, and even more affected when CHARLES DICKENS and JOHN RUSKIN joined his critics.

George Meikle Kemp was a fascinating character. He always gave the impression that he was waiting for something awful to happen and he suffered from strange melancholy moods. For him, the criticism of his design was painful.

However, the jeers died down after a while and Kemp seemed almost happy as his brainchild raised its presence in Princes Street.

That's why his friends were shocked to hear, in March 1844, that he had gone out for an evening stroll and vanished! A few days later, his body was recovered from a canal ....

The SCOTT MONUMENT

Did George fall in by accident? Or was he pushed? Did he commit suicide? There are no answers.

Two years later his son set the final stones on the now famous Edinburgh landmark—the now very famous Scott Monument.

FIND
THE
LADY

IT cannot be said of many people that they have had three funerals. But it has been said about Lady GRANGE. She was the spouse of JAMES ERSKINE of GRANGE who was Lord Justice Clerk in the 1730s. Both James and his brother, the Earl of MAR (who was a leader in the 1715 Jacobite Rising) were staunch Jacobites.

The consensus of opinion from those who knew Lady Grange, seems to be that she was a strident-voiced, flyting virago. Her husband was, on most occasions, the target of her scorching tongue. The matter which often sent her into a tempestuous tantrum was her husband's allegiance to the Jacobite cause. She herself was totally opposed to the Stuart claim to the British throne. Her chances of winning the argument were always slim, but her behaviour eventually earned her a 'red card' and she was removed from the field of play!

On one particular daft night at the Grange Edinburgh home, some Jacobite conspirators were doing a bit of plotting with her husband. Lady Grange, without being detected, had wriggled under a sofa in the room where the gang had met. From this hide, she was enjoying an evening of glorious eavesdropping.

Alas, the outrageous things those plotters were saying finally got her goat and she yelled out her annoyance, threatening to expose them! Immediately, her husband and his henchmen grabbed the lady, and within an hour or so, she had been unceremoniously bundled off to the Isle of Skye! There the MCLEODS held her in an old hut until they passed her on to the MCDONALDS in Uist.

Meantime, back in Edinburgh, news of the lady's death was deliberately spread far and wide. Her 'grieving' husband attended her mock funeral at Greyfriars Kirkyard.

The story continues that the McLeods took her back from the McDonalds and banished her to the island of St Kilda for seven years. After that, in case her place of imprisonment had become generally known, she was shipped back to Uist again!

The poor lady died in 1745, but some daft folk thought that even in death she might betray her enemies. So, a coffin filled with turf was the centrepiece of her second mock funeral at Duirinish this time.

And, at the same time, her body was

being taken to her third, and *real* funeral.

Lady Grange was finally laid to rest at Trumpan on Ardmore Bay in Skye.

But can this elaborate and painful operation of concealment—spread over 14 years —really be believed? Were such excessive actions necessary just to save the skins of a few Jacobites? Or was it just the ploy of James Erskine to rid himself of an unbearable, scolding wife without actually killing her?

JOHN
THE
TWO-FACE
MOLE

WHAT an undesirable character was JOHN
SMOLLETT of Dumbarton! Surely others of
that respected family would have disowned
him. They were shipowners and merchants,
trading mostly with the Western Highlands
and Islands.

Such business was not exciting enough
for John. Honest folk in the West of
Scotland would have dubbed him a man
capable of pawning his granny's walking
stick. He certainly got up to some shady
ploys.

The political turmoil of the late
sixteenth and early seventeenth centuries
provided a lovely play-park for bold John.
The Scottish Lords chose him as an undercover man during the reign of JAMES VI.
He fed them all kinds of juicy information.
At the same time, he was a mole for Queen
ELIZABETH's faction and, indeed, was even
involved in a plot to kidnap King James!

The silver edge to his tongue gained
him friends in high places and they were
the people who eventually rescued him

The SPANISH ARMADA
from a TAPESTRY *in the* HOUSE OF LORDS

from the hangman, or from rotting in jail
for his misdeeds. Smollett's career, however,
was destined to sparkle with even more
spectacular events.

He became very friendly with LACHLAN,
chief of the MCLEANS of Duart. And he
and Lachlan became very friendly with the
crew of a ship at that time rocking gently
at anchor in Tobermory Bay during the
summer of 1588. It was the famous Spanish
galleon which had taken refuge there after
the defeat of the Armada.

Lachlan, in fact, had got so chummy
with the Spaniards that he hired a hundred
of them to help him fight the MCDONALDS!
It was John who saw to it that the Spanish
mercenaries were not over-paid.

Now, as that summer mellowed into
autumn, an almighty explosion ripped

through the galleon. It became an inferno from bow to stern in a matter of minutes. Only 18 of the complement of 400 men survived the holocaust.

Rumours whispered that Smollett and Lachlan had done the dirty deed, intending only to damage the ship and lay its treasure bare. They hadn't meant to blast it out of the water!

Well, so much smoke and dust was swirling that even yet there is no clear view of that day's events. Did the two rascals really light the fuse? Was there any treasure on board that ship? Was there, as another rumour suggests, a second Spanish Galleon in the Bay which torched the first? If so, why? Will the truth ever emerge from the silt below those waters?

MORTIMER
REALLY
IS DEEP

IONA may be number one in the list of Scotland's ecclesiastical islands, but surely Inchcolm—the 'Iona of the East'—in the Firth of Forth is a close second.

Folktales tell how, five or six centuries ago, people of substance queued up to book their burial places on the island. Indeed Shakespeare, in the play *Macbeth*, refers to SWENO, the Norse King, pleading and paying to have his dead Vikings buried on Inchcolm. So it is clear that the place was well thought of.

But there was one purchaser of a burial place on Inchcolm who surely had a raw deal. He was Sir ALAN MORTIMER of

The ABBEY *of* INCHCOLM

Aberdour. This saintly knight gave large gifts of money and land to the monastery of Inchcolm and in return was granted the right to be buried in the Abbey church.

Alas, when this great man died, his remains fell victim to a gang of monks who were a right handless lot! It was arranged that Sir Alan's body would be conveyed from Aberdour to Inchcolm by barge, and a group of monks were employed to crew the craft.

But those incompetents handled that barge like children playing boats in a paddling pool! They were about half way along the deep channel which reaches from near the Fife coast to the island, when the swell on the Firth revealed that they had not properly secured the great lead coffin to the deck ... it began to slide ... they couldn't hold it ... into the dark waters it plunged with a huge splash and ghastly gurgles! When the waves settled, the monks knew that the casket had gone forever.

Those hapless men with wet habits were responsible for that channel in the Firth of Forth ultimately being called 'Mortimer's Deep'. But, questions remain. Was it an accident? Or was it a plot? Did somebody think the knight unworthy of burial on the Sacred Isle? And is he *really* down there? The firth holds on to its secrets ....

THE
STRANGE TALE
OF THE
SLEEPY
MINISTER

AROUND about 1745, quite a few communities in the Black Isle were leaning towards the Episcopalian persuasion. This fact tended to undermine the comfort and confidence of Presbyterian ministers in the area.

Although the Revd DONALD FRASER was a strong preacher and lavished his care and attention upon the folk of his Killearnan charge, it seemed that his congregation just did not quite take to him. And yet, when he received a call to the neighbouring parish of Urquhart, he said that he would not go if even *one* man, woman or child in Killearnan asked him to stay. Alas, not one soul in the parish put forward such a plea.

Now, it was around about this time that a strange affliction overtook Donald Fraser. He found that on Sunday mornings, somewhere between the singing of the first psalm and the prayer, he would fall fast asleep in the pulpit! His explanation for this phenomenon was that two local women had taken a spite against him. This caused them to make a clay figure of him which they stuck all over with pins! They then placed the figure on a dunghill! They were, of course, witches, and by this nasty piece of sculpture, had settled a spell upon him. Thus he got soporific after the psalm.

How embarrassing it was to have the beadle shake the minister awake and tell him to get on with the service!

When the Revd Fraser was asked why the two ladies had picked on him, he replied, 'I think it was something I said .... ' But a notion had been given an airing in the parish that perhaps the minister's sleepiness was the result of 'measures' he was taking to fortify himself against a dreadful feeling of sagging confidence. Was he perhaps partaking of spirits which were less than Godly to help him face a rather unfriendly congregation?

Perhaps it is not surprising that, at his new Urquhart charge, he got on famously with the membership and his sleepy Sunday morning spells completely disappeared.

The so-called 'witches' of Killearnan were not burned at the stake and, in spite of guessing games and conjecture, the mystery of the minister's dozy spells still hangs over the area.

WAS
SERGEANT
DONALD McLEOD
FOR REAL?

STORIES are still told in the North and out on the Islands about Sergeant DONALD McLEOD. He was born at Ullinish on Skye in 1688—the midwife at the birth could not possibly have guessed that the helpless creature she had brought into the world would prove to be Scotland's answer to a real-life 'Superman'.

McLeod's *Memoirs* were written for him by an assistant minister from Perthshire. WILLIE THOMSON, however, stopped being an assistant minister when he committed some misdemeanour which disqualified him from following that profession. Thomson later met up with McLeod in London.

McLeod's childhood was a painful experience for him. His father ran away and deserted the family. Donald, forced to live with his nasty old grandfather, eventually escaped to join the Royal Scots.

He fought against the Old Pretender at Sheriffmuir in 1715, where indeed he kill-ed a dragoon, but not before the dragoon's sword split Donald's skull open! This was when the lad from Skye first displayed his Superman traits. He wrapped a handkerchief round his head to hold his skull together and carried on with the battle!

In 1745, he received a musket ball through his leg at the Battle of Fontenoy where the British, Dutch and Germans fought a draw with the French. Again, this didn't stop our Donald!

Out on the Plains of Abraham in 1759, Donald McLeod suffered multiple wounds helping General WOLFE to defeat the French commander, MONTCALM de ST VERAN. Fate was to deal thus with those three men— Wolfe was killed, Montcalm was mortally wounded, but Donald survived, yet again. In fact, he came back home from Canada on the same ship that carried the body of General Wolfe.

Much later, at the age of 90, Donald McLeod, the hero of Skye, was shipwrecked and washed up on the Yorkshire coast. He appears to have been saved by tying himself to a plank of wood!

After that, he was to become a Chelsea Pensioner and, in London, he met up with his biographer—Willie Thomson.

McLeod's fascinating story further reveals that, in interludes between battles, he married several times and fathered 16 sons.

When his *Memoirs* were finally written, he was 103 years old, his oldest son was 83 and his youngest was 9!

McLeod of Skye lived out the rest of his life on a meagre pension and no record can be found of his last resting-place—neither in Scotland nor in London. What happened to Donald McLeod?

Indeed, his life is so unbelievable, it is tempting to wonder whether the larger-than-life Donald McLeod ever existed!?

THE SCARPERING CLERICS TOOK LOADS OF HISTORY

The man called JOHN LESLIE certainly led a charmed life. He was Canon of Aberdeen, Senator of the College of Justice and Bishop of Ross from 1565 until 1596—although he wasn't in Ross for much of that time.

The ill-fated MARY Queen of Scots was glad of his friendship, and it is said that he was actually at the Palace of Holyrood on the night the Queen's musician, DAVID RIZZIO was murdered.

He may have survived that rough interlude, but later he was put into the Tower of London by Queen ELIZABETH for merely being one of Mary's fellow-travellers. But

The ruined CATHEDRAL *at* FORTROSE

John's charisma went to work again and he was released without even a slap on the wrist. Off he went back home to his magnificent Palace of Fortrose.

Surely he must have hated saying goodbye to it when, a few weeks later, he made his escape to Rome from his enemies in Scotland. He took with him the archives of Fortrose Cathedral which preserved not just great chunks of local history, but national history too!

The Bishop of Ross lived at the Vatican as the guest of the Pope for three years before he was appointed Vicar-General at Rouen.

It is likely that those Cathedral archives are resting in some forgotten corner of the Vatican. But where? And have any Scots

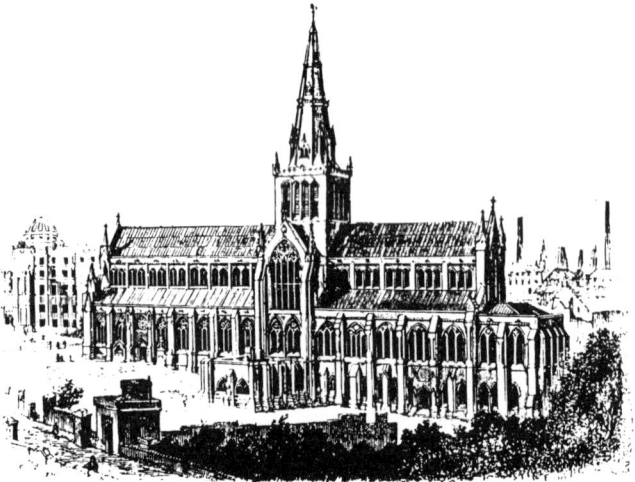

GLASGOW CATHEDRAL *from the* SOUTH EAST

historians gone to look for them? Perhaps scholars are too shy to ask permission to search.

Of course, John was not the first cleric to 'do a runner' with valuable archive material. Back in 1560, Archbishop JAMES BEATON fled from Glasgow Cathedral in the face of angry Reformation mobs, and what a collection of historic bric-a-brac he took with him! The mobs did a fair bit of vandalising in the Cathedral themselves, although posterity is grateful that the great church itself escaped destruction.

Beaton packed his bags four weeks before the Scottish Parliament declared the Reformed Faith to be the new national religion. He took priceless ornaments, the original burgh charter of the city, the historical records of the Cathedral and even some of St Mungo's bones! The Archbishop 'body-swerved' his enemies and disappeared. He eventually turned up in Paris and his treasure trove was off-loaded into the Scots College there.

It is possible that some, or *all*, of those precious objects were destroyed during the French Revolution. But, perhaps not! If not, then where are they now?

Who would like to begin the search?

A
MYSTERIOUS
BRAIN
DRAIN

SCOTLAND has gifted the world with a *cornucopia* of home-bred riches, and not least among her gifts has been a selection of the finest human brains. One of these brains belonged to JAMES CRICHTON of Eliock whose intellectual brilliance sparkled in the second half of the sixteenth century.

This mastermind would never have had to say 'pass' to any question ever put to him on 'Mastermind'. Indeed, St Andrews University acclaimed him as one of the brainiest scholars who had ever graced that venerable seat of learning.

Crichton became tutor to JAMES VI, and, no doubt, groomed the young monarch for his big job—uniting the kingdoms.

Later Crichton became a soldier in the French Army—a prodigal waste of the colourful grey matter this lad had to offer!

By the age of 20 he had mastered Latin, Italian, French, Greek, Flemish, Hebrew, English (of course!), Chaldaic, Spanish and German. He took philosophy, mathematics, theology and astrology in his stride, and somehow acquired a thorough knowledge of the Cabala—a secret Hebrew philosophy which is said to have been passed on from one mind to another by word of mouth!

James Crichton had an amazing memory and was exceedingly handsome. His skills with every sort of weapon, and as a dancer and horseman, were breathtaking. Indeed, he must have been the kind of person to make ordinary folk feel absolutely sick!

In Italy, his spreading fame brought new challenges. There he was given the opportunity to gather the professors of Padua University around him and tie them up in philosophical knots concerning their interpretations of Aristotle!

The Duke of nearby Mantua chose James as tutor for his son ... but, from this point on, the story gets murky.

Europe was shocked to learn that, shortly after the appointment, James, a swordsman of some repute, had been killed in a brawl! Another story claimed that he had been murdered by his pupil! But nobody has been able to lift the shroud of mystery covering the secret of how death came to this extraordinary Scotsman.

Writer JOHN JOHNSTON, in his *Heroes of Scotland* published in 1603, called James 'the Admirable Crichton'.

THE
JAMES TAIT
LEGEND

THERE really was a Revd JAMES HILL TAIT —minister at Aberlady Parish Church from 1861 until 1877, Chaplain to the Royal Company of Archers, the Sovereign's Bodyguard in Scotland. But, when his exploits are recounted, some folk may think he is a figure of fiction.

His arrival at Aberlady coincided with the settlement of an argument which typified the long-running rivalry between two great local families, the WEMYSS family and the LUFFNESS family—both landed gentry.

A new manse was to be built for the new minister, and Wemyss wanted a bathroom included. Luffness thought it was nonsense to give a minister a bathroom, and opposed it. Wemyss won the day. The bathroom was built in the end, but Wemyss had to fork out the money for it.

Tait seems also to have argued about the site of the manse, not wanting it to be too accessible—he wanted a little privacy from time to time—but it was built where the heritors wished it to be, in the grounds of the kirk.

The minister hit back by having the builder add on a vestry which was not in the original plans. He won that particular encounter because the work was too far advanced before anybody noticed!

Now, James was an enthusiastic golfer and a top-class archer. Legend has it that he challenged the celebrated Scots golfer, TOM MORRIS, to a round, but said, 'Tom, you use your ordinary clubs, but would you mind if I use, not my golf clubs, but my bow and arrows?!' Morris agreed, and off they went round Aberlady golf course.

Betting was heavy on Morris. The great golfer played textbook golf and seemed non-plussed by the accuracy of Tait's arrows which flew in beautiful curved flight up the fairways, onto the greens, and into the holes! It was as close a match as anyone could have wished for, and what a surprise the villagers got when the minister won— by a single arrow!

The local bookie laughed all the way to the bank!

The minister would regularly play real golf with Earl Wemyss, and would always let his lordship win—which ensured Tait an invitation to lunch.

One time James had the opportunity to

go on holiday to Egypt and announced his masterplan for the visit. He would take a 'Morris 28' golf ball with him and drive it eastwards into the desert, using the Grand Pyramid as a tee! Then, he said, at some future date, when the lettering on the ball had been faded by the weather, a passing archaeologist would find it and misread the words as 'Moses 28'. The considered opinion then of the finder would be that Israel's great leader played golf!

The minister returned home from Egypt claiming that he had, indeed, played his historic golf shot. But, perhaps James Tait was just a joker?

Did a golf ball ever hit the desert? Or were all these tales merely invented by other jokers to swell the legend of this grand eccentric?

THE
MYSTERY
OF THE
NAPIERS'
WEE ROOM

EVEN those of us who could never really get the hang of logarithms at school, would surely marvel at the brain that could invent them. That brain belonged to JOHN NAPIER who, legend has it, was a wizard.

He took after his dad, Sir ARCHIBALD NAPIER, the owner of Merchiston Castle on the outskirts of Edinburgh. Sir Archibald seems to have been even more of a wizard than his son. He held the public office of Master of the Cunzie House—which was the Mint—and because of some amazing metallurgical experiments he carried out there, he was deemed by some to be a wizard.

JOHN
NAPIER

Archie could even forecast the future. He had said that MARY Queen of Scots would escape from Loch Leven Castle before the 5th May 1568. The Queen's captors couldn't have been listening, however, for she tip-toed out of her imprisonment on 2nd May!

Was Sir Archibald really a wizard? Or

had he other means of getting early warn-
ings on future moves in the affairs of state?

When he built Merchiston, the plans
included a secret room which was reached
by the narrowest stairway in Scotland. The
room was directly above the Oak Room, a
lounge where his guests would foregather
and partake of plentiful supplies of the
host's claret and brandy.

The most important and powerful
people in Scotland were regular guests at
the Castle. In the Oak Room, confidential
matters of state were gossiped about,
especially when tongues were well lubri-
cated. Juicy pieces of information floated
around that room, ripe for the taking. Sir
Archibald, however, never appeared to be
paying much attention—he was too busy
making sure his guests' glasses never drain-
ed dry.

MERCHISTON CASTLE

Years later, those in the know said that he always had a servant stationed in the secret room above, to write down every word that floated upwards when the high and mighty were chatting together—surely an early form of bugging device!

Therefore, armed with all these vital secrets, did Sir Archibald later hold them over the heads of his guests like the proverbial Sword of Damocles? Perhaps his reputation as a prophet is quite unfounded?

His other son, ALEXANDER, inherited Merchiston. This lad was a right tearaway! He once hi-jacked his school—Edinburgh High School—and smashed the place up! On another spree, he threw a man called HEPBOURNE down the Tolbooth stairs while the Court of Session was sitting. In spite of the victim's injuries, Alex got away with it!

He was ultimately knighted and became a Lord of Session. In this capacity, he had plenty of time to indulge his favourite pastime of astrology. Sometimes it is wondered whether Alex perhaps owed his immunity to retribution, and his remarkable success in life, to his astrology. Or was it to the judicious use of his father's secret room?

DID HE
REALLY DIE
WITH A
GIGGLE?

SCOTLAND has always had a plentiful supply of good brains. Some of them have become more famous than others. One of the finest, and indeed, more famous, was surely that of Sir THOMAS URQUHART, who lived through the middle years of the seventeenth century.

He was educated at King's College, Aberdeen, and liberal though his training was, he could never take a tolerant view of the Covenanters. After several abortive attempts to quell the upstarts in the north, he fled from Cromarty to London where King CHARLES I made him a knight.

Charles, of course, lost his head in 1649 and Thomas, for his loyalty to the King, was put in jail. But not for long. His contemporaries were amazed when OLIVER CROMWELL, quite unexpectedly, set him free.

Thomas was a poet, historian, eccentric humourist and a wizard with words. He devised a universal language which he called LOGOPANDECTEISION! It had 11 genders and each word was as significant backwards as it was forward! It certainly provided a wonderful facility for anagrams!

He also wrote a book in praise of the Scottish nation called *The Jewel*, but his greatest literary achievement was the translation of the French satirist, Rabelais. Indeed, some said he had *improved* the Frenchman's work with some devastating slang of his own!

Thomas Urquhart remained a Royalist in spite of it being such an unfashionable stance. But he managed to keep his head below the parapet while Cromwell was about and, indeed, he became so successfully invisible that the last years of his life are shrouded in mystery.

The report of his death, however, is interesting. It is said that when news came through to him of CHARLES II's restoration to the throne, he suddenly went into a fit of uncontrollable laughter—and promptly died!

WAS
RAVI
A SPY?

ONE last great fling of fun and sparkle
before the world would change forever—
that's how some older folk, looking back,
describe the magnificent 1938 Empire
Exhibition, held in Bellahouston Park,
Glasgow.

It was of Hollywood epic proportions
and thirteen and a half million people
visited it in six months—in spite of every
Saturday being wet, in spite of the place
being closed every Sunday, and in spite of
the grim Munich triumph of ADOLF
HITLER over NEVILLE CHAMBERLAIN during
that eventful year. Barely ten months after
the exhibition ended, the world was to be
changed forever by the outbreak of the
World War II.

During the winter before the Exhibition,
it was difficult to visualise a Wonderland
arising out of that vast quagmire of a
building site. But there was a low buzz of
excitement among the workforce. Most
were aware they were building a magic
show—a special part of Scotland's history.

The team on the construction of the United Kingdom Pavilion were drawn from many parts of the world—Scotland, of course, and Ireland, but also from Jamaica, New Zealand, Italy and Canada.

There was one particular bricklayer's labourer called RAVI. He spoke a kind of shattered English and would say only that he was from mid-Europe. His name was pronounced 'ravi', as in 'ravioli', and he seemed to enter into the fun as his Glasgow mates tried, unsuccessfully, to imitate his accent. Ravi was accepted as a cronie and was soon drinking Friday night pints with his workmates in the pubs along Paisley Road.

One man in the squad always held Ravi at arm's-length, however. He was SAM WALLACE, the drain man. Sam was rather concerned by Ravi's activities during meal-breaks—Sam was the only one who seemed to notice what the mid-European was doing.

The drain man had been shadowing Ravi, and he claimed that the foreigner was scribbling notes and making wee drawings of the various buildings which were being erected. According to Sam, Ravi was paying particular attention to the building of the Tower of Empire—THOMAS TAIT's Tower which, up on Bellahouston Hill, dominated the Exhibition. Sam had no doubt Ravi was

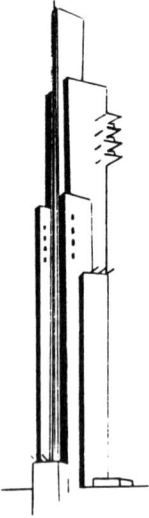

a German spy recording all the information he could in preparation for the War that Sam said was certainly coming.

Suddenly, Ravi vanished. He didn't say goodbye and no trace was found of him at the address where he said he was living. Indeed, nobody there had ever heard of him. Further mystery was added when two men in grey suits came on to the site looking for Ravi. They left without saying why they wanted him.

TAIT'S
TOWER

Was Ravi really a spy? Or did he perhaps owe someone a lot of money? Was he in fact being chased by secret agents or debt-collectors?

Tait's Tower was pulled down before the War was declared. It certainly never guided any German bombers ....

WHO
WAS THE
LITTLE
GIRL?

CENTRAL Scotland was covered in white
frost when 10th December 1937 dawned.
By mid morning, a bitter wind threatened
snow. Just after lunch, the sky darkened and
the street lights came on. The snow came
down in blizzardy gusts. Winter had come
a wee bit early that year.

The first twinges of unease about the
future were beginning to be felt by ordinary
people. They had enjoyed the splendour of
the Coronation of King GEORGE VI and his
Queen, ELIZABETH. The newspapers and
cinema newsreels reported every detail of
the royal spectacle. But they also brought
news of Japan's invasion of China ... and of
the dismay felt in Britain when the Duke
and Duchess of WINDSOR decided to visit
that friend of Japan, ADOLF HITLER, in
Germany.

As the year ended, people wondered
what the future would bring. Even though
Christmas was soon, there was definite
foreboding in the air.

It was felt especially on that dismal

Friday in December, when the news broke in the early evening of a serious rail crash on the Edinburgh–Glasgow line at Castlecary. Folk reacted as if they had been expecting a disaster. A train had run into the rear of another which was stationary due to snow interfering with the signals. Thirty-five people died.

Rescue work was agonisingly difficult due to the dreadful weather conditions and the mangled state of the carriages.

One particularly harrowing story haunts this tragedy. An exhausted rescue worker asked later if anybody had found the little girl. He said that at the height of the struggle to free victims, he had glanced through to the other side of a carriage and had seen, walking past a shattered window, a little girl who seemed to be dressed only in her nightgown ... he dashed round the end of the carriage thinking she would perish in the freezing temperature. But when he had struggled through, she was nowhere in sight! She had vanished. He made a frantic search along the length of the train, but he couldn't find her.

Other rescue workers later claimed to have seen her, but the girl in question was never traced. Her name did not appear on the casualty list, nobody reported her missing. Who—or *what*—was that wee lassie?

A
WHALE
OF A
TIME

IN the middle of last century there was little consideration for the preservation of any of the species which had inherited the earth—or the sea. Nobody blubbered at the killing of whales—they were an excellent source of income and would be plentiful forever. Amazingly, some whales survived the massacre for many years. One is still talked about in Dundee and Bo'ness. And those two Scottish ports had plenty of whales to talk about in those days.

Bo'ness whalers, round about the middle of last century, used harpoons made by the local blacksmith, WILLIAM CUMMINGS. He produced the best. In the season of 1853, JOHN MCKENZIE, one of the star whaling men of the East Coast, had a William Cummings harpoon which became his favourite. That year, he caught a record number of whales with it. He dreamed of hanging it on his kitchen wall, as a trophy, when his whaling days were over.

It was one day, late in the season, when John spied one of the finest specimens of this gigantic mammal he had seen in a long time. As if guided by radar, his harpoon unravelled its rope in a perfect arc and the point buried deep into the high back of the monster. The chase was on!

John's craft was pulled at the speed of light as the whale careered away in its attempt to shake free. But it seemed like another huge catch for the Bo'ness whaler when, suddenly, the rope snapped! The whaling boat shuddered with the recoil, and the great whale sped off with the harpoon sticking from its back like a flagpole, the length of rope trailing behind. To say the least, John was not best pleased!

The story goes that, 40 years later, the same whale was caught by a Dundee whaling man. The harpoon was still sticking into its back, bearing the manufacturing marks of William Cummings of Bo'ness. John McKenzie, by then retired, identified the instrument as his favourite whale-stabber of 1853!

John didn't take it home. He left it at Dundee Museum. But, what about the whale? What kind of life had it endured through those forty years? Was it shunned by its fellow whales? Did it provide a great backscratcher for itchy whales? And why was that whale able to escape capture for so long when it carried its own targetmarker?